Building
Additions in Steel

The Architecture
of Vertical Extensions

Building Additions in Steel

The Architecture
of Vertical Extensions

Daniel Stockhammer, Astrid Staufer,
Daniel Meyer (eds.)
ZHAW Zurich University of
Applied Sciences
Institute of Constructive Design

With contributions by Jürg Conzett
and Roger Diener, Lorenzo De Chiffre,
Yves Dreier, Patric Fischli-Boson,
Patric Furrer, Matteo Iannello,
François Renaud, Martin Tschanz

PARK BOOKS

7 Acknowledgments
Oya Atalay Franck

9 Foreword
François Renaud

11 Vertical Extension as Concept and Construct:
From an Ideal of Completion to Reforming
Existing Structures
Daniel Stockhammer

COMPOUNDING OF EPOCHS

22 Geneva—for Centuries, an Experimental
Laboratory for Vertical Urban Development
Yves Dreier

38 New Construction Dressed in an Old Coat:
Philipp Jakob Manz's "Lightning Architecture"
for the Salamander Shoe Factory in
Kornwestheim, 1927
Daniel Stockhammer

PROCESSES OF REPLACEMENT

52 Constructing Vertical Extensions—
Reassessing Italian Postwar Modernism
Matteo Iannello

64 Design through Constructive Thinking:
The Extension of the Faculty of Architecture
in Hannover by Friedrich Spengelin and
Horst Wunderlich (1961–1966)
Daniel Stockhammer

TECHNOLOGICAL EUPHORIA

82 The Psychology of the High-Flyer—
On the Vertical Extension of Vienna
since Deconstructivism
Lorenzo De Chiffre

94 Taming the Future in the Tube:
The Design for the Extension of the Kunst-
akademie Düsseldorf by Karl Wimmenauer,
Lyubo-Mir Szabo, and Ernst Kasper in 1968
Martin Tschanz

REDISCOVERY OF METAMORPHOSIS

112 *Forme forte* and the Picturesque Manner of
Vertical Extension at the Turn of the Millennium
Patric Furrer

122 History of Mining, Mining of History:
The Design for the Reconstruction of the
Zollverein Coal Mine, Shaft XII
Jürg Conzett and Roger Diener

HOW TO BUILD ON?

136 Ways towards Ambiguity and Multivalence
Astrid Staufer

156 On the New Potentials of Steel Construction
Patric Fischli–Boson

Acknowledgments

Oya Atalay Franck
Director, School of Architecture, Design and
Civil Engineering at ZHAW

The School of Architecture, Design and Civil Engineering at ZHAW in Winterthur is the oldest professional school dedicated to the construction sector in Switzerland. It owes its identity to this tradition, as well as to its orientation towards current and future demands in architectural and engineering education.

In this sense the school sees itself as a motor for the further development of a future-oriented building culture in teaching and research in the context of continually changing conditions in practice. In collaboration with partners from the professional world, current themes are actively engaged with. Existing and new questions from building practice and social and technological conditions are proactively investigated, and innovative processes set into action.

This requires bold future vision along with constant, critical reflection on traditional approaches. The prerequisite for this is to know tradition, to be aware of it—only in this way can it be continually reconceived and newly interpreted, as a critical basis for the creation of high quality and dignified, human-oriented living and working spaces.

This publication thematizes these requirements in reference to a specific mode of building, steel construction, in a specific context, that of building extensions. This small book delivers a large, truly beautiful contribution to this discourse. Our thanks thus go to the authors and the Institute of Constructive Design (Institut Konstruktives Entwerfen, IKE), and especially to the Swiss Center for Steel Construction (Stahlbau Zentrum Schweiz, SZS).

Foreword

François Renaud

For centuries the European city has known the phenomenon of the vertical extension or vertical renovation. Until the razing of city fortifications in the first half of the nineteenth century, this was an obvious means of expanding the stock of living and working space. In the context of present discussions on urban densification, vertical extension has gained new currency.

This publication, the result of a collaboration between the Institute of Constructive Design and the Swiss Center for Steel Construction, bears the title *Building Additions in Steel—The Architecture of Vertical Extensions,* directing our attention towards vertical extensions of houses. In addition to an introduction and overview, this publication contains eight chapters, each concerning a research question, a realized or an unrealized project. The time period within which the projects considered are situated spans from the interwar period to the turn of the twentieth century.

As the school's former director, Stephan Mäder, observed in the preceding publication, *At Home in Steel: Residential Construction in Steel— Thoughts on Space and Structure,* the IKE has always been interested in difficult, apparently unattractive themes and questions within building practice. With few exceptions, current practice presents the vertical extension as the realm of wooden construction. The impression has been created that only wooden construction methods are suitable for erecting the structural framework quickly, easily, efficiently, and sustainably. Industry organizations, political demands, and technical innovations have really reinforced this rather one-sided perception.

From where does this interest now come to investigate the potential for steel in vertical extensions? Is this another difficult and apparently unattractive inquiry? Is this a decisive matter or not?

The research-based development of architecture deals extensively with design components, and primarily consists of continually formulating fundamentally new questions and of taking the necessary time, perhaps arriving at unexpected answers, but in any case good solutions, not just the correct ones. The unbiased engagement with questions that are insolvable in principle gives architects the freedom of choice and allows them to assume the responsibility for decision making. The chapters within *Building Additions in Steel* expand the field of vision, and open up research questions that may provide valuable and inspiring support for intelligently expanding aesthetic aspects of the structural engineering repertoire of vertical extensions.

Vertical Extension as Concept and Construct

From an Ideal of Completion to Reforming Existing Structures
Daniel Stockhammer

One of the biggest challenges of our time is the qualitative densification and continuing development of existing residential structures. Sustainable development means the renewal and upgrading of existing buildings. The reconstruction and continuing development of concepts is no longer a question of idealism, but instead of resources and economics.[1] The most ingenious extensions are able to enhance the qualities of pre-existing structures without diminishing their impact.

The vertical extension of existing structures represents the most sophisticated strategy for urban densification. Vertical extensions and steel construction, meanwhile, have long been closely associated: from the late nineteenth century until the early twentieth century, the history of vertical extensions was the history of steel construction. Already inscribed in this history, hence, is a relationship of tension between architectural ideals and constructive possibilities.

DYNAMICS AND IMPULSES IN THE TWENTIETH CENTURY

Changing fundamentally in tandem with the industrial manufacture of steel and the continuing development of the material, of manufacturing and construction technologies, were the conditions for the concept of the vertical extension:[2] the addition of stories again becomes an economic argument. Performance capacity with regard to weight reduction, span widths, and assembly time soon begin to call into question inherited certainties regarding building practices. What became possible here is the vertical extension that avoids burdening the substructure, and a building process that does not hinder existing utilizations. The thinning of the mass through the deployment of steel building technology allows the free design of vertical extensions. At the beginning of the twentieth century, technical progress and the constructive possibilities were far ahead of the architectural ideals of tradition and handcrafted work. The invention of steel construction enabled the vertical

Enhancement of existing structures: the all-metal aircraft G38 by Hugo Junkers, Dessau, in 1929 (above) with sufficient load capacity for additional loading. The same aircraft after the addition of a passenger cabin in 1931 (below). The continuing use of the pre-existent was not a question of idealism, but instead of resources and economy.

The compounding of epochs: a "new whole" as a result of the extension and "smoothing out" of building styles, illustrated here by a downtown hotel in the early twentieth century. The Grand Hotel Fürstenhof in Nuremberg in 1912 (above) and after the addition of a vertical extension by the architects Ludwig Ruff and Georg Richter 1928 (below). Thanks to multistory trussed girders and the punctual load transfer via new supports within the old structure, the replacement and upgrading of the old attic level was possible without interrupting operations.

extension and the "smoothing out" of building styles from the nineteenth century (see the first section of this publication, "Compounding of Epochs," pp. 20-49).

After World War II, the paradigms of modernity were displayed through an ostentatious display of structures in steel and concrete; now being demonstrated was the replacement of the pre-existent and a break with the past. To be sure, the constructive principles of the prewar era were barely altered in steel building, while pre-existing structures were nonetheless declared to be the pedestals, now burdened by history, for the architecture of a new time. The variety of approaches both before and after the war can be illustrated in an exemplary way by the vertical extensions of two hotels from the *Gründerzeit* era. In the Berlin of the 1950s, for example, Paul Baumgarten saw himself confronted—like his colleagues Ludwig Ruff and Georg Richter in the Nuremberg of the 1920s—with existing building stocks dating from historicism, whose weight-bearing capacity was not suitable for additional loads. In both instances, the planners decided for a steel framework consisting of lattice girders which spanned the old building like a bridge, carrying the loads punctually via new supports within the existing building. While Ruff and Richter clad their framework with a massive façade and fused divergent building styles into a new whole through the ideal of stony monumentality (figs. 3, 4), Baumgarten sought a sharp division between old and new through the aestheticization of steel construction (figs. 5, 6).[3] During the 1950s and 1960s, nonetheless, through architects like Baumgarten, the process of replacement remained the result of a painstaking confrontation with pre-existing architecture. Characterizing the epoch of vertical extensions during the era of German reconstruction was a respect for existing façade orders and supporting structures—generally for reasons of economy (see the second section of this publication, "Processes of Replacement," pp. 50-79).

Observable during the 1960s through an increasing abandonment of the "functional city" and the new promises offered by the materials and building industries was a genuine technology euphoria. Concerns about the environment and a delirium of technological feasibility lead, among other things, to enormous plastic bubbles or systems of tubes suspended above the rooftops of cities. Vertical extensions become genuine protective zones with adjustable atmospheres—reservations for nature and people, who were to be sheltered from deleterious influences with the help of the latest technology. And although the projects by Karl Wimmenauer in Düsseldorf or the Viennese architectural scene around the Haus Rucker Co must be regarded as protests or utopian visions, their technoid construction stands for the reconquest of the "densified city." A confrontation with the existing city and its architecture—for example concepts for the vertical extension "Il Monumento Continuo" by Superstudio (fig. 8)—serve as trailblazers for the rediscovery of existing architectural stocks (see the third section of this publication, "Technological Euphoria," pp. 80-109).

Separation from the past: Hotel am Zoo in prewar condition (above) and after its vertical extension in 1956–1957 by Paul Baumgarten (below). Employed for the supporting structure was the same concept used in the hotel extension by Ludwig Ruff and Georg Richter in Nuremberg (fig. 4). In contrast to the latter, Baumgarten uses the exposure of the steel construction to emphasize the modernist ideal of the overcoming of historicism.

Vertical extension as reinterpretation and transformation: seven additional stories in steel construction on Rue Jouffroy-d'Abbans in Paris, La caisse d'epargne de France by Édouard Albert, 1954–1956. A new bel etage facilitates views through to the historic building. "Under these conditions, it was difficult to achieve the cohesive unity of the new structure [with the old one]. The interlocking of old and new has the effect of a curiosity, and not so much as an organic and logical combination." Benedikt Huber, "Aufstockung eines Geschäftshauses in Paris: Architekt Edouard Albert," in *Das Werk* 44 (1957), no. 11, pp. 382–383, here p. 382.

Observable with the waning of the twentieth century was a rediscovery of the object. From the outside, Roger Diener's vertical extension project for the Zeche Zollverein, for example, appears as the continuation of the architectural volume in glass form. The interior structure of the vertical extension, however, takes the form of a reactivation and further development of the existing steel supporting structure. Thanks to Jürg Conzett's intelligent supporting structure, the potential of the old structure is activated and elaborate strengthening measures for the existing structure are spared. The Vienna roof structure by Delugan & Meissl too can be characterized as a transcription of the existing façade in the form of a vertical elevation. Here, the principle of the window and balustrade strips is translated into a sculpture of folded bands; choice of materials and coloration maintain a connection to the old building from the 1960s. In the late twentieth century, the theme of the rediscovery and updating of constructive and design principles leads toward the concept of metamorphosis (see the fourth section of this publication, "Rediscovery of Metamorphosis," pp. 110-133).

CONSTRUCTIVE CONCEPTS REGARDING
VERTICAL EXTENSIONS IN STEEL

Virtually no other building task has been determined as decisively by the principles of load transfer and supporting structure as the vertical extension of existing buildings. According to Konstanty Gutschow and Hermann Zippel, who authored one of the earliest investigations into conversions and extensions, the most important task here is "to minimize the weight of the supplementing stories as far as possible."[4] As early as the 1930s, they attempted to subdivide vertical extensions in exemplary "cases," which—depending respectively upon the load-bearing capacity of the substructure, the weight of the extension, and the construction line—have retained their validity as principles up to the present day.[5] Reconstructed and illustrated in an exemplary fashion in the discussions of specific buildings (text contributions by Jürg Conzett with Roger Diener, Martin Tschanz, Daniel Stockhammer) are three basic structural principles of vertical extensions in steel.

FIRST PRINCIPLE:
LOAD TRANSFER OUTSIDE OF THE EXISTING BUILDING STRUCTURE

This principle of the support structure is applied when the existing parts of the building have already been optimized with regard to their requirements and are unable to absorb new loads. In some cases, moreover, ongoing operations within the substructure need not be disturbed. The vertical extension therefore proceeds on the basis of an autonomous, external system of supports. Where more than one story is involved, there is often a recourse to a system using tie rods (truss posts) in place of central supports; these carry the weight of the new floors to the external supports via the roof trusses. A clamping of these external supports and the reduction of their buckling length is achieved through punctual anchoring on the existing façade. Often, these

Rediscovery of the "densified city": reactivation of the pre-existing architectural substance in Superstudio's design for the Grand Hotel Colosseo.
Photomontage (1969) as part of the conceptual work "Il Monumento Continuo."

Renewable architecture and the rediscovery of construction: the residence Zur Linde (former pub) in the rural neoclassicism of the 1880s, Tös-Brunnadern, St. Gallen. The special extension of the half-timbered building is translated into a two-story vertical extension consisting of 2 × 4 lattice girders. Each of the new stories is rotated by 45 degrees and adapted to the geometry of the pavilion roof. The loads are transferred via four contact points to the lower supports and in the existing structure via four supports which lie behind the outer wall and are inserted through the floor slabs. Photomontage, extension project, Ermatinger Residence, 2011, architect Daniel Stockhammer.

supports rest on their own point foundations, which commonly have a frictional connection to the existing foundation. This principle of an external load transfer is illustrated by a deepened investigation of the Salamander Shoe Factory in Kornwestheim by the office of Philipp Jakob Manz (see also the text "New Construction Dressed in an Old Coat" in the first section of this publication, pp. 38-49).

SECOND PRINCIPLE:
LOAD TRANSFER VIA PARTS OF THE EXISTING BUILDING STRUCTURE

In these examples, only individual parts of the existing substructure can receive additional loads. Serviceable here in many instances are the external walls, which are generally less loaded in relation to their thicknesses in historic buildings than internal walls and supports. If the external walls of the building are stable to such an extent that they can receive the entire additional load, then the loads are—as with the first principle—absorbed by steel trusses which span the entire building and transferred to the perimeter walls via external supports. Here as well, construction work can usually proceed without hindering ongoing operations. This principle was used by Friedrich Spengelin in Hannover, where he suspended a steel grid (as a new floor in place of the old ceiling) from steel trusses with tie rods, which transfer the load to the outer walls via supports (see the text "Design through Constructive Thinking" in the second section of this publication, pp. 64-79). Included here as well is the extension of the Zeche Zollverein by Roger Diener and Jürg Conzett. Thanks to the additional loads of the extension, Conzett achieves a preloading of the existing steel girders, thereby elevating their loadbearing capacity. The new loads are diverted via the existing external supports (see the text "History of Mining, Mining of History" in the fourth section of this publication, pp. 122-133). Alternatively, buildings may be given a new or strengthened core (consisting of support systems or wall segments), which is extended from the foundation through the entire building; for example the extension of the HPP research building at ETH Zürich by the architects Andreas Ilg and Marcel Santer and the engineer Daniel Meyer (p. 148, figs. 18-20).

THIRD PRINCIPLE:
LOAD TRANSFER THROUGH THE EXISTING BUILDING STRUCTURE

Here the substructure is stable to such a degree that it can receive the new loads of the extension securely and transmit them underground. Particularly exemplary here is the "load distribution" of the extension project for the Kunstakademie Düsseldorf by the architect Karl Wimmenauer and the engineer Stefan Polónyi. Here, sixty filigree supports "perforate" the existing roof and transfer the additional weight to as many existing capstones as possible by means of sole plates or supports (see the text "Taming the Future in the Tube" in the third section of this publication, pp. 94-109).

The rediscovery and investigation of such outstanding examples are intended to contribute to the reconstruction of knowledge about an extraordinarily important theme in building, albeit one that has to date received too little attention—both for architects as well as for researchers. This focus on steel construction, coupled with a categorization according to constructive and architectural principles, forms a new approach to building tasks, and in way that may lead toward a new basis for further development. The present work is not a conclusion, but instead an opening toward research into concepts concerning the reactivation and continued narrative of existing architecture.

1　　See Uta Hassler, "Umbau, Sterblichkeit und langfristige Dynamik," in Uta Hassler, Niklaus Kohler, and Wilfried Wang (eds.), *Umbau: Über die Zukunft des Baubestandes* (Tübingen/Berlin: 1999), pp. 39–59.

2　　On the decisive continuing development of steel construction between 1880 and 1940, see Ludwig Beck, *Die Geschichte des Eisens in technischer und kulturgeschichtlicher Beziehung. 5. Abtheilung: Das XIX. Jahrhundert von 1860 bis zur Gegenwart* (Braunschweig: 1903); Siegfried Giedion, *Building in France, Building in Iron, Building in Ferroconcrete* [original edition 1928], new edition with an afterword by Sokratis Georgiadis (Oxford: 1996); Ekkehard Ramm, "Entwicklung der Baustatik von 1920 bis 2000," in *Der Bauingenieur,* 75 (August 2000), pp. 319–331; Wieland Ramm, "Über die Geschichte des Eisenbaus und das Entstehen des konstruktiven Ingenieurbaus," *Stahlbau,* 70, no. 9 (2001), pp. 628–664; Joachim Scheer, "Entwicklungen im Stahlbau – gespiegelt an 75 Bänden der Zeitschrift 'Bauingenieur,'" in *Der Bauingenieur,* 75 (August 2000), pp. 332–341.

3　　In their initial designs, Baumgarten still envisioned the preservation of the central roof ridge façade; for the sake of a clear separation from the existing structure, however, he opted for its demolition instead. See Annette Menting, *Paul Baumgarten: Schaffen aus dem Charakter der Zeit* (Berlin: 1998), pp. 168–196.

4　　Konstanty Gutschow and Hermann Zippel, *Umbau: Fassadenveränderung, Ladeneinbau, Wohnhausumbau, Wohnungsteilung, seitliche Erweiterung, Aufstockung, Zweckveränderung. Planung und Konstruktion. 86 Beispiele mit 392 vergleichenden Ansichten, Grundrissen und Schnitten* (Stuttgart: 1932), p. 28.

5　　Ibid., pp. 28–31.

INTRODUCTION

COMPOUNDING OF EPOCHS

Geneva—for Centuries, an Experimental Laboratory for Vertical Urban Development

Yves Dreier   p. 22

New Construction Dressed in an Old Coat: Philipp Jakob Manz's "Lightning Architecture" for the Salamander Shoe Factory in Kornwestheim, 1927

Daniel Stockhammer   p. 38

1 Over the years, Geneva grew to be the most densely developed
   city in Switzerland: various epochs of vertical development along
   the Place de Saint-Gervais in Geneva, 1914.

COMPOUNDING OF EPOCHS

Geneva—for Centuries, an Experimental Laboratory for Vertical Urban Development

Yves Dreier

When it comes to urban densification via vertical extensions, Geneva is considered a trailblazer for many metropolises today. But what is special about this tradition? What are the characteristic features of Geneva's "vertical urbanization"?

THE HISTORY OF VERTICAL EXTENSIONS IN GENEVA

The historical background for the Genevan practice of vertical extensions of buildings was the massive stream of French Huguenots during the sixteenth and seventeenth centuries, in conjunction with the preservation of the restrictive ring of the city wall (demolished only in 1860). No horizontal expansion of the urban space occurred. Another factor is the circumstance that in the course of history, Geneva was spared massive destruction of its historic architectural substance.

Still surviving in the quarter of the Rues Basses around the Temple de la Madeleine, as well as near the Church of Saint-Jean, are some of the very early vertical extensions, some of which date back to as early as 1640. Today, they offer insights into the methods of constructions employed at the time. Clearly, the existing development was consolidated and expanded via various vertical and other extensions, and the utilizations of the buildings were diversified through the insertion of large glass windows in the uppermost floors. This made possible the installation of small watchmaker's workshops, the so-called *cabinotiers*. Over a period of three centuries, the medieval two-story development was extended vertically by up to four stories.

Within Europe, this historic process made Geneva an exemplary instance for vertical extensions of existing buildings. And this construction tradition continues up to the present, making Geneva the most densely developed city in Switzerland.

2 Geneva in the early twentieth century: the Place de Saint-Gervais as an exemplary instance of urban densification.
3 Planning instrument for possible densification: the Geneva cartography of potential vertical extensions.

COMPOUNDING OF EPOCHS

Necessary for a better understanding of this phenomenon in urban development is the genesis of Geneva's building regulations.[1]

A CARTOGRAPHY OF THE VERTICAL EXTENSION

The most recent building regulation of 2008 grants additional building rights for all parcels in individual zones—without distinctions regarding previous utilizations. With the aim of evaluating the potential for new living space, the city elaborated a cartographic survey intended to encompass all of the possibilities of vertical extension. For reasons related to the protection of historic monuments, the greater portion of buildings from the nineteenth and early twentieth centuries were excluded from this inventory. Buildings erected after 1945 are regarded almost without exception as suitable for vertical extension.

This survey yielded a theoretical increase of approximately 10,000 apartments. Evoked by the new registration is a utopia of urbanization that does not involve architectural decisions being made from case to case; instead, the question of the expansion of existing building stocks is approached within a larger framework. A legally regulated upward expansion through vertical extensions harbors the possibility of a unified urbanistic conception that encompasses the entire city: with main traffic arteries being singled out for a maximal growth in height for existing buildings; with building complexes whose extensions respect their urbanistic and architectural formal languages; and with individual buildings designed to fill existing gaps between buildings. The practical implementation of such a vision, however, emerges as far more difficult.[2] By their very nature, it is a question with vertical extensions of highly individualized construction measures that are adapted to individual buildings. In addition to the need for an expert assessment provided by the responsible building commission, as well as an opinion from the Commission des monuments, de la nature et des sites (CMNS) concerning an insertion into the respective architectural surroundings, the project must also be structurally and economically feasible. Architecturally, each individual buildings must be approached with great sensitivity: it needs to be taken into account that until the end of the nineteenth century façades were articulated by cornices and decorative elements, while twentieth-century architecture tends to be characterized by clear proportions and a renunciation of ornamentation. Heterogeneous building stocks permit greater freedom when planning extensions, while with more homogenous architectural ensembles the vertical extension of an individual building must be considered carefully. In streets with buildings dating from various epochs, it becomes necessary to weigh their respective historical and art-historical significance in such a way that a harmonious overall impression emerges.[3]

This brief summary of the relevant aspects already shows that the Geneva cartography permits a variety of interpretations, and suffers, despite all of its visionary powers of persuasion, from a lack of tangible criteria for determining the buildings for which an added superstructure comes into question. There is also an absence of individual proposed solutions. But ownership status too complicates a collective design approach, so that this cartography provides little more than a reference value. Its lack of urbanistic stringency, moreover, reduces the vertical extension to a purely quantitative potential. In order to exercise a sustainable influence on the future of Geneva's cityscape, it must be transformed into a vertical development plan—the only instrument capable of formally defining the intended appearance of the building under proposed construction. Only with such a plan can urbanization processes address the question of densification through vertical extension in qualitative terms as well.

CRITERIA OF URBANISTIC AND ARCHITECTURAL EVALUATION (ABCD METHOD)

Despite these shortcomings, the Geneva cartography of vertical extension raises a series of important questions. Guided by the intention of preserving the unity of the eave heights along streets, or at least ensuring a respectful approach to the maximum eave height in force up until now, it provides a fresh look at Geneva's architectural microstructure and permits a detailed analysis of its morphological peculiarities. A desire for increased control led to considerations concerning the question of how urbanistic undertakings could be oriented more emphatically toward qualitative criteria. The new approach demands proposals for solutions which also integrate the environment of the individual building under consideration for extension, while at the same time furnishing the authorities with general criteria of evaluation for authorizing building applications.

The so-called ABCD Method[4] defines four reference areas, each assessed in relation to morphological criteria: A/ the district, B/ the building ensemble (built surface), C/ public and private space (open areas), D/ the individual building.[5] Because the method focuses on urbanistic questions, it allows considerable leeway for architectural concepts—whether in consonance with or through a deliberate withdrawal from the existing context. The focus is thus shifted from a discussion concerning permissible eave heights to the quality of the pedestal building of the planned vertical extension. The emphasis of the investigation is both on a cross-section of the spatial situation in relation to street and inner courtyard, as well as a longitudinal section of the altered impact on the immediate vicinity. Instead of an exclusive preoccupation with permissible heights, the architects are encouraged to undertake a comprehensive examination of the respective building project and the specific conditions of the extension.

We must distinguish two categories in relation to which the ABCD Method leads to objective, differentiated results: on the one hand, there is the punctual vertical extension of the building within a dense, continuous urban texture, with the intervention being restricted to just a few apartments that are arranged around a staircase. On the other, there is the vertical development of an ensemble in a more open urban texture which manifests no direct connection to neighboring buildings and which encompasses a large number of apartments which are grouped around multiple vertical axes.

The degree of architectural sensitivity required to successfully link a vertical extension with the pedestal building seems to be inversely proportionate to the number of apartments under development. A smaller project which closes a gap or attempts to set a new urbanistic accent emerges as more difficult than a large-scale project involving vertical extensions for an entire complex of buildings. Leading to difficulties with large projects, conversely, is the process of coordination with numerous residents regarding the adaptation of infrastructural elements—laundry and basement rooms, parking places for bicycles, the placement of waste containers, boiler rooms, elevators. To say nothing of considerations concerning the necessary redesign of entrance spaces in the lower levels. A necessity in projects with such dimensions, moreover, is a redefinition of the residential quality of the district as a whole. This also applies to green spaces, storage systems, street areas, and local transport, service provisions, parking spaces for automobiles, motorcycles, and bicycles, as well as local supply chains.

EXAMPLES OF VERTICAL EXTENSIONS

The following five examples of recently realized vertical extensions are intended to exemplify characteristic approaches to the search for solutions in Geneva. These case studies shed light on the potential of the newly gained space, while illustrating the diversity of possible architectural solutions.[6]

The office of BASSICARELLA is responsible for the new cornice story of a structure at the corner of the Place du Cirque/Rue Bovy-Lysberg, which is characterized by a highly precise analysis and reinterpretation of its embeddedness in the surrounding architecture. The emphasis on continuity is also apparent in the mineral materiality of the prefabricated concrete, as well as the elegance of the details. Unusual as well is the office concept of this structure.

Situated directly at the edge of the Parc Saint-Jean is the high-rise of the Fédération des Entreprises Romandes, which was vertically extended by François Maurice and Giorgio Bello, and which is characterized by its thoroughgoing imitation of the existing building and its original proportions. This steel-and-glass architecture, with its shimmering, copper-colored façade, thereby underscores the character and status of the building as a solitaire.

At the corner of Sentier des Saules/Rue des Deux-Ponts, Brigitte Jucker-Diserens designed the vertical extension of an old factory whose buildings had already been built on a number of times. The newly added structure accommodates two large apartments, and its opulence signals a lack of concern with the surrounding urban architecture.

The three-story vertical expansion by Raphaël Nussbaçumer on the Avenue de Sécheron offered an opportunity to reconceive the façade structure of the original building, erected in 1958. The new volumes encompass four interlocking apartments whose windows display subtle displacements

4, 5 Continuation of a building tradition: vertical extension at the Place du Cirque in Geneva by BASSICARELLA Architectes, 2011.
6, 7 The main headquarters in the high-rise of Fédération des Entreprises Romandes in Geneva, built in 1964–1966 by François Maurice and Jean-Pierre Dom, before and after its refurbishment and vertical extension in 2007 by Giorgio Bello and Aydan Yurdakul, in collaboration with the original architect François Maurice.

in relation to the existing grid. A two-story vertical extension allowed Jacques Bugna to insert a building complex between Rue Barthélémy-Menn and Rue John-Grasset. The infrastructure of the district was extended to include a nursery school on the ground floor. The metal-clad edge of the vertical extension contrasts clearly with the concrete façade of the pre-existing structure.

STRATIFICATION AS A METHOD OF URBAN DENSIFICATION

These vertical extensions are components of Geneva's urban renewal and they testify to a political will to see through vertical densification in the outskirts as well, as prescribed by the *Plan directeur cantonal 2030* (PDCn). As a response to the need for additional housing, extending existing structures offers an alternative to the designation of new, lower-value building zones and to displacing the population beyond the city limits, where, in the municipalities, building sites are more numerous, building codes are more generous, and construction costs are lower.

In relation to Geneva, this means that vertical extension must be grasped as an intellectual task, one that exceeds the narrow framework of the building regulations that must be adhered to. The *Loi sur les surélévations* of 2008 altered the urbanistic approach, stimulating thinking within new categories. It is no longer simply a question of closing various gaps between buildings, but instead of using the roof as a new building site: the roof surface becomes a land resource that is located up above our heads.[9]

The idea of a building on top of the building is entirely consistent with the spirit of the *Loi fédérale sur l'aménagement du territoire* (LAT), which is directed against a further expansion of the city in surface area, and which calls for the restrained utilization of land: the law channels spatial development toward already developed urban areas, and favors densification via successive development. Playing a role as well are the requirements of the Cantonal Master Plan, which seeks to reestablish equilibrium between work and residential spaces, and whose aim is to alleviate the housing shortage, with special weight being accorded to a social balance within districts.[10] Vertical extension plans must be disentangled from the restrictions of the *Loi sur les démolitions, transformations et rénovations de maisons d'habitation* (LDTR), which envisions only residential utilizations. With a discreet wink in the direction of the traditional *cabinotier*, and of course with the restriction that direct juxtaposition must not be allowed to diminish quality of life or create insoluble points of conflict: the creation of commercially usable

8 Investigation of the possibilities of densification in Geneva: potential map for vertical extensions by Cecilia Juliano, master's thesis (EPFL, 2014).

surfaces high above the existing buildings would certainly benefit the city, endowing apartment buildings with a somewhat mixed character. In certain areas, these extensions could also be made available for common utilizations, thereby enhancing social contact between residents. Greater freedom regarding utilization could resolve numerous problems which pertain to staircases, building technology, and ancillary costs.[11] Up to now, efforts toward increased flexibility have encountered a number of obstacles,[12] preventing the use of vertical extensions as an opportunity to improve the energy balance of the building, or for the long-term securing of higher standards or the elaboration of new typologies.

VERTICAL URBAN DEVELOPMENT

Vertical urban development is an expression of a vision of symbiosis between city and architecture in which building-on epitomizes the continuity of the urban structure.[13] Since vertical extensions have the power to alter the character of a street, the equilibrium of a block of buildings, or the physiognomy of an urban district, they contribute to anticipating the city of the future. As a centuries-old Geneva tradition, extension consistently relies on the inherent potential of existing building stocks. In a contemporary context, characterized by short-term thinking, we rarely see planning based on more extended timeframes, i. e., in such a way that individual architectural experiments are capable of merging successively to form a vision of the city of tomorrow. To be sure, the effective period of building regulations extends through many decades, and every building possesses its own rhythm of transformation, with an average time period of thirty years between necessary refurbishments. With approximately one hundred new apartments being created by vertical extensions annually, it will take an entire century before the potential of the law is comprehensively implemented. The city, which is something more than an aesthetic, heritage-listed object worthy of preservation, continually develops in this growth process, absorbing the structural excrescences of an epoch, along with its resistances. This capacity for appropriation is an argument for allowing a constant and dynamic evolution, which can also be punctual and fragmentary.[14]

Vertical urban development is based on the harmonization of the streetscape through the alignment of eave heights and a qualitative densification of the city. In this pursuit of a formal coherence of the overall ensemble, the architecture remains restrained and urban while attempting to establish strong connections with the existing context and meanwhile also maintaining architectural unity. Since it can hardly be seen as desirable to crown the city by stacking mutually contradictory architectural solutions on top of one another, the ironic citation of building types must remain an exception among vertical extensions, and must be reserved for a small number of prominent buildings.

In the face of the excesses of particularism and individualism in our epoch, we must remain vigilant, according sufficient attention to the coherent, homogenous cityscape, as formulated as an ideal in modernism. While

9

10

9, Simulation of a vertical extension of the urban fabric with an
10 additional story. Photomontage study, Canton of Geneva, 2007.

fragmentation and diversity may be of value regarding relationships between individuals and their environment, the striving for homogeneity and cohesion in relation to the overall cityscape nonetheless retains its justification. In a city like Geneva, which is characterized by the growing obsolescence of its architectural inventory, vertical urban development must also aim toward the renewal of the lower stories, and this through a gradual upgrading that would be unattainable at the desired level of quality through regulations alone.

The analytical approach of the ABCD method is based on the idea of a gaplessly developed, compact and homogenous city. Since vertical extension calls for a stratification within which epochs and styles are mixed together, it must be perceived as indebted to the mimetic principles of building in existing contexts.[15]

In the framework of the implementation of the *Loi sur les suréléva-tions,* the Canton of Geneva prepared photomontages that compare current with future building heights from the perspective of the public street space. The photomontages extend the existing façades in faithfully detailed copies up to the legally permitted heights. This procedure of a simple lengthening—naïve to be sure, and hardly to be regarded as a realistic image of the future—abstracts architectural modes and punctual interventions, and conveys the impression that the added stories might not have a disturbing impact on the quality of the public street space. In addition, Geneva has at its disposal a two-dimensional digital land registry, as well as a model of the entire urban district on a 1:500 scale. These two means of representation complement one another, and allow concrete examinations of the sunlight exposure and of the volumes of the planned buildings.

Nonetheless, the actual impact of vertical extensions on the city remains difficult to predict. For good reason, as well as by virtue of the invention of specific working and monitoring tools, Geneva is regarded as an experimental laboratory for vertical urban development—which testifies not least of all to the city's ambition to preserve a characteristic, centuries-old peculiarity of its architectural fabric.

---

1   In 1895, with the adoption of an initial law that restricted the eave height of each building to a maximum of 21 meters, Geneva supplied the framework for further urbanization. This not only predetermined the future potential for densification; municipal building regulations were also oriented toward contemporary standards with regard to hygiene and aesthetics. In 1929, the introduction of various building zones reaffirmed a maximum eave height of 21 meters for downtown zones, at the same time prescribing a height dimension that was proportional to the width of the street. The coefficient 2/3, still valid today, is based on the notions of hygiene and construction possibilities that prevailed at the time, and restricted vertical extensions in narrow lanes and for buildings in rear courtyards, ensuring that natural light would be admitted into the lower levels as well. In 1961, the *Loi sur les constructions et installations diverses* (LCI) raised the maximum eave height for the city center zone (Zone 2) to 24 meters, and to 21 meters for the suburban district (Zone 3). The possibility of adding stories ushered in a new phase of vertical extensions, and led to a wave of demolitions and new constructions. The *Loi sur les surélévations,* abbreviated to L 10088, entered into force in

2008, and today allows a maximum height of 30 meters in Zone 2 and 27 meters in Zone 3. The gain of two stories in already highly densified districts led to an increase of vertical extensions. This impetus to construct a new town above the town is however being checked some extent by the *Loi sur les démolitions, transformations et rénovations de maisons d'habitation* (LDTR), intended to promote the affordability of apartments, which froze rents for a period of five years. This regulation, which entered into force in 1992, and which has been adapted continuously to the development of rental prices, reduces the profitability of new vertical extensions, and puts a brake on the attractiveness of demolitions and new constructions through the obligation to increase the number of rooms in new building 1.5 times. See Immanuel Malka, *Loi L10088: Densifier par la surélévation. Une analyse des opportunités et obstacles liés à l'augmentation des gabarits en zone II et III à Genève,* Master's thesis (Zurich: 2016).

2　Pierre Bonnet, *Évaluation des raisons de la sous-exploitation des surfaces constructibles à l'intérieur des gabarits actuels* (Geneva: 2007).

3　Buildings at crossings or forking streets have the character of urbanistic visual points of rest. When it comes to the choice of an upper terminus for a building, the decision between a penthouse solution or a roof with dormers is often a question of belief. The vertical extension cannot be permitted to interfere with the admission of natural light into the lower stories. Interior courtyards are to be upgraded as urban spaces.

4　Bruno Marchand and Christophe Joud, *Étude et méthodologie ABCD* (Geneva: 2016).

5　Valid here are the following guiding principles: A/ An analysis of the district underscores its peculiarities within the urban texture and, in this framework, specifies the significance of the building to be extended. B/ For each building that belongs to a larger ensemble, a certificate must be produced which demonstrates that its planned vertical modification gives due consideration to the immediate vicinity. C/ Open or undeveloped space is regarded as a common good, and is to be protected from particular interests and from negative effects associated with an altered eaves height. D/ With the design of the vertical modification, respect for the qualities of the existing building and its relationship to neighboring buildings must be foregrounded.

6　Carole Westhoff, *La surélévation: définition d'une problématique,* énoncé théorique de projet de master EPFL (Lausanne: 2013).

7　For André Corboz, for example, the *piano nobile* of ducal buildings in Italy of the fifteenth and sixteenth centuries was an expression of the hierarchical layering of city and society. By means of bridges and galleries between buildings, these new architecture levels also served at times as a network of routes, and transcended the hitherto existing urban texture through new urbanistic structures that mirrored a changing political, economic, and social order.

8　See Steven Beuc, *Opération superposition* (Lausanne: 2012).

9　In his research into the *ville spatiale,* Yona Friedman turns his attention toward a critical examination of our relationship to the urban context and to the land. His microstructures liberate themselves from the previous existing constraints of the city, and open a path toward a redefinition of human relationships. His reinterpretation of the natural environment of human beings as a culturally shaped "layer" endows his concept with great symbolic power, transforming it into a universally usable model.

10　Found in the "high-rise city" of Ludwig Hilberseimer is a triple vertical layering: in terms of traffic/transport through the separation of flows; structurally through the stacking of levels; programmatically through the division of utilizations. His architectural language unifies horizontal strips and periodically interrupted surfaces, in accordance with the respective function. By rendering them legible on a number of interpretive levels, as building, district, and city, this dialogue of forms not only enriches the urban composition, but also the spatial and social experience of the city.

11　In his manifesto *Delirious New York,* Rem Koolhaas elucidates the vertical layering of the modern metropolis with reference to the Downtown Athletic Club. Various elements are positioned along a longitudinal axis that is defined by the elevator, whose invention in the 1870s revolutionized architecture. The mixing and hierarchization of activities becomes a social condenser—and an apotheosis of modern metropolitan life.

12　To name just a few difficulties: complicated legal and political framework conditions, high building costs, a lack of profitability which is aggravated by loss of rental income during conversion work, the requirements of heritage listing, problems with access for individuals with restricted mobility, the maintenance of security standards, the necessary subsequent improvement to structural features, multiple owners.

13　According to Bernard Huet, architecture must not develop at the expense of the city, but must instead rely upon a sensitive interplay of a variety of forces and simultaneous developments. The perspective of vertical urban development is founded on the premise of equilibrium between harmony and complementarity. Moreover, a practice of vertical extensions that is adapted to the building ordinances of the respective city harbors the possibility of reconciling city planning and architecture with one another. See also *Avenir suisse, Élever la ville* (Zurich: 2008).

14　Mélanie Goldschmid, *Densifier Genève face au patrimoine moderne,* mémoire de master EPFL (Lausanne: 2009).

15　Patrick Rérat (ed.), *Géo-Regards: revue neuchâteloise de géographie,* no. 1 (2008): *Reconstruire la ville en ville.*

New Construction Dressed in an Old Coat

Philipp Jakob Manz's "Lightning Architecture" for the Salamander
Shoe Factory in Kornwestheim, 1927
Daniel Stockhammer

Gründerzeit-era buildings and changing user demands have been in conflict with one another since long before today's densification strategies. As a "commitment of great value and an impediment to further development,"[1] the architectural inventory of historicism was regarded as a potential mortgage as early as the early twentieth century. The addition of stories—as the vertical extension of the principles of classical order—became a touchstone for architects as well as engineers. The task today is to reconstruct their building expertise as a substrate for new solutions, as an object lesson for constructive building in existing contexts in between old visual ideals and new demands.

In 1928, a supplement to the structural engineering magazine *Der Stahlbau* contained a detailed report about a vertical extension which sought to master precisely these challenges while "conforming fully to operational requirements," and which was nonetheless "generally beneficial to the external appearance of the building":[2] the expansion of the Salamander Shoe Factory by the office of Philipp Jakob Manz. According to the contemporary specialist press, the project "[…] presented certain difficulties whose overcoming may be exemplary for similar tasks."[3] As a commendable instance of vertical extension, it appeared shortly thereafter in one of the first basic reference works on the theme of conversions.[4]

VERTICAL EXTENSION AS AN ECONOMIC AND CONSTRUCTIVE CONCEPT

In the early twentieth century, the industrialization of shoe fabrication in Kornwestheim and its successful expansion allowed the Jakob Siegle & Cie. Salamander-Werke to become the largest shoe factory in Germany (fig. 2). The streamlined corporate management required the planning of the new construction to ensure optimal operationality, as well as time efficiency and a fixed budget.[5] At that time, only few planning offices were large or experienced enough to offer these kinds of guarantees for the construction of facilities of this magnitude. In 1903, with Philipp Jakob Manz (1861–1936) from nearby Stuttgart and his specialization in industrial building, the company had found its new architect.[6] Erected just one year later under his supervision was the so-called "Hundred Meter Building"; the first large building at the new production location in Kornwestheim, directly on the main thoroughfare and the train tracks. The core idea of the design is a completely freestanding rectangular plan measuring 197 × 15 meters for a flexible organization of production operations. Externally adjoined "extremities" contain the staircases and wet rooms (fig. 3).

In 1927, when further land purchases fell through due to the high prices demanded by property owners, it was decided for reasons of economy to instead add two stories to the Hundred Meter Building and an adjacent courtyard wing that measured 76 meters.[7] The expansion had to proceed rapidly, while not exceeding the cost of a horizontal extension or interfering with ongoing operations inside the buildings. A preliminary study of the state of the buildings and of operational procedures was therefore indispensable. Once again, Manz was entrusted with the planning work.

The interior supports were strong enough to absorb the payloads of the first additional story. The payloads and dead loads of a further story, however, could not be absorbed by the interior supports or the existing exterior walls. The new loads would have to be transferred to the outside of the existing walls. Manz opted for the principle of standoff mounting and suspension. Here, the roof trusses (A in the axonometric rendering) utilize tie rods (B) to capture the payloads and dead loads of the uppermost story and transfer these to independent supports (C) outside of the façade. In order to reduce buckling height, the new supports are anchored back into the existing façade pilasters, so that the force transmission into the building site proceeds via punctual foundation reinforcements. This external load transfer resulted in an enormous advantage for the logistics of shoe fabrication: the first additional story (3rd upper story) offered a continuous production surface measuring nearly 3,000 square feet that was free of supports and access elements. The new floor was mounted on the old roof. Set on the existing roof girders at the same time—on a substructure designed to level out the old roof inclination—were semicircular "Zores steel sections";[8] a self-supporting construction which, as a "lost formwork" with a covering in lightweight concrete, became a stiff panel (D). The new slab between the two new added stories consisted of prefabricated hollow slabs suspended between the steel girders (E).[9] The roof trusses were clad in so-called hollow-core planks, i. e., lighter hollow slabs in pumice concrete. These form both the horizontal ceiling cladding of the uppermost story as well as the external inclined roof covering (F). Sheets of tar-free cardboard as the uppermost roof layer provide a seal (G).

"THE PRINCIPLE OF RAPID BUILDING":
TECHNOLOGIZATION OF THE BUILDING
PROCESS

The construction of the vertical extension can be understood as a material realization of Manz's principles: a simple, calculable, and optimizable building system combined with a rapid serial-production process. Since prefabrication and dry construction stood in the foreground for the sake of cost-efficient implementation, steel emerged as the optimal building material. The project explanation of 1928 emphasizes that building additions in steel enjoyed a decisive advantage: "There, the possibility of a straightforward inspection of [existing] load-bearing capacity immediately provided a clear picture concerning the admissibility of supplementary loading, an advantage of steel construction that weighs quite heavily in the event that no plans from earlier constructions are available. For the vertical extension itself, [...] steel may be the only available and economical building material, in particular given the brief construction schedule desired [...] which would not [have been] even remotely attainable with any other building material."[10]

The principle of fast, cost-effective building soon earned Manz a reputation as a "lightning architect."[11] Developed especially for the project, for example, was a mobile crane that facilitated a division of labor and serial montage that approaches assembly-line work. Wooden beams positioned tightly along the outer wall and between the ceiling joists of the existing roof formed the support for the mobile crane; consequently, strengthening measures in the old building became unnecessary. Step-by-step, by means of this lifting device, the delivered steel frames—section by section—were hoisted (fig. 1). The external mainstays were placed in advance on the new point foundations and anchored there. Finally, the joist for the new suspended ceiling was set into place, on which the upper supports and the roof trusses were erected. While the manufactured steel frames were secured by the purlins and wind bracing (H), the crane was shifted one section further. As the crane began with the assembly of the succeeding frame, work then shifted towards the roof cladding. From there on out, the façade and finishing work could continue in parallel and in dry conditions. The existing stair tower was elevated by two levels, and supplemented by an additional story at the southern end. The speed with which the montage of the 273-meter vertical extension was accomplished is confirmed by the brief construction schedule: the office of Manz received the commission from a factory in Saarbrücken on July 26, 1927, and launched construction operations on August 24, just one month later. At the end of September, just eight weeks after the contract was awarded, work had already been completed.[12]

OLD IMAGE WITH NEW MEANS

Steel remained a purely constructive, not a design element; the use of exposed masonry work for its protection therefore seemed obvious. Paradoxically, it was the new technology (steel construction) that made the extension of the earlier image ideal (solid brick masonry construction) possible in the first place.

For Manz, to be sure, the primary focus was on technical and financial optimization, but by no means did he disregard questions of a project's outer appearance. Here, architectural qualities are to be found—alongside the spatial flexibility of an "open" layout—in the treatment of the representative side of the façade. For Manz unified the outer shell with the existing brick façade so skillfully that old and new did not appear as two separate parts, but instead as a new whole.

The original three-story façade was dominated by powerful, story-height masonry pillars (fig. 4). In the vertical fields between them, the expansive window surfaces are separated by balustrades executed in a variety of designs. The window lintels of the uppermost row of windows are given round arches and serve as optical termini of the fields. Above, a cornice and turrets round off the building above. Manz exploited the new external supports, executed in steel, in order to extend the façade. He continued them vertically, together with the brick cladding, through an additional story. While this to be sure caused the proportions of the pillars to appear more slender, the earlier image of a colossal order was nonetheless preserved. The "doubling" of the pillars also reinforced the depth of the façade, and, according to the specialist press, "[…] strongly benefit the building's outer impression."[13] Manz terminated the new four-story main façade with a powerful cornice. The uppermost, fifth story is set back (hence the offset of the steel supports on the new main ceiling beam inward by approximately 45 centimeters (I)), underscoring and extending, as an attic story, the idea of the classical order—and this despite the fact that a certain purification was introduced by the removal of historic elements.[14] "After the conclusion of building work, no distinction between the extension and the 'old buildings' was recognizable,"[15] in the judgment of one contemporary (fig. 5).[16]

The skillful application and extension of the "column of orders," to cite Goethe's remarks concerning the extensions of the Palazzo della Ragione in Vicenza, has always been regarded as the "major problem" that "confronts all modern architects."[17] The way in which some artists succeed, as here, in combining new and old, so that "the tangible presence of his creations makes us forget that we are being hypnotized," is compared to "the power of a great poet who, out of the worlds of truth and falsehood, creates a third whose borrowed existence enchants us."[18]

For Philipp Jakob Manz, a precise study of the existing architecture was essential to planning. But it was only a knowledge of constructive principles and spatial concepts from building history that allowed him to achieve a coherent expansion of the complex. It was in the reconstruction of knowledge, in its adaptation and further development, that Manz discovered the constructive solution to the vertical extension of the Salamander Shoe Factory.

1 Uta Hassler, "Umbau, Sterblichkeit und langfristige Dynamik," in Uta Hassler, Niklaus Kohler and Wilfried Wang (eds.), *Umbau: Über die Zukunft des Baubestandes* (Tübingen/Berlin: 1999), pp. 45–46.

2 No author, "Fabrikerweiterung der Salamander-Schuhfabriken J. Siegle & Cie.," in *Der Stahlbau*, 1 (1928), pp. 9–10.

3 Ibid., p. 9.

4 Konstanty Gutschow and Hermann Zippel, *Umbau: Fassadenveränderung, Ladeneinbau, Wohnhausumbau, Wohnungsteilung, seitliche Erweiterung, Aufstockung, Zweckveränderung. Planung und Konstruktion. 86 Beispiele mit 392 vergleichenden Ansichten, Grundrissen und Schnitten* (Stuttgart: 1932), p. 94.

5 Franziska Schneider and Georg Schmelzer, *Industriearchitektur im Wandel der Zeit: Schuhfabrik Salamander Kornwestheim* (n. p., presumably 1985), p. 3.

6 Sources for the work of Philipp Jakob Manz are extremely meager; an estate no longer exists. His residence in Stuttgart was destroyed in World War II,

and the estate of the office was evidently disposed of by his heirs. See Petra Bräutigam, *Mittelständische Unternehmer im Nationalsozialismus: Wirtschaftliche Entwicklungen und soziale Verhaltensweisen in der Schuh- und Lederindustrie Badens und Württembergs,* PhD thesis, Universität Tübingen (Munich/Oldenburg 1997), pp. 59–64.

7 See Schneider and Schmelzer, *Industriearchitektur im Wandel der Zeit* (see note 5), pp. 9–11.

8 The so-called Zores steel sections are semicircular iron profiles, also known as "fer arrondi," which are especially suitable for absorbing horizontal forces: they are "[…] given the same cross-section, they have a somewhat reduced tensile strength against bending compared to double T irons. In contrast, they have the advantage of greater stiffness in relation to forces which act from the sides." From: "Die sogenannten Zores-Eisen (schmiedeiserne Tragbalken)," in Emil Maximilian Dingler (ed.), *Polytechnisches Journal* (Augsburg: 1869), pp. 273–274.

9 Together, prefabricated ceiling elements in reinforced concrete, consisting of an upper and lower panel with cross pieces in between for the sake of weight reduction, form a stiff ceiling panel. The employed "hollow reinforced-concrete block slab ceiling" is designed for a load capacity of 400kg/m². Gutschow and Zippel, *Umbau* (see note 4), p. 94.

10 See Paola Barbera, "Messina despuès del terremoto del 1908: nuévas técnicas y lenguajes antiguos," in *Actas del Noveno Congreso Nacional y Primer Congreso Internacional Hispano-americano de Historia de la construction* (Segovia: 2015), vol. I, pp. 177–187.

11 Bräutigam, *Mittelständische Unternehmer im National-sozialismus* (see note 6), pp. 59–64.

12 "Fabrikerweiterung" (see note 2), p. 11.

13 Ibid, p. 10.

14 Disappearing with the extension work, as shown by a comparison of historical images, was the historicizing design of the central stair tower, the old cornice, the avant-corps and turrets, as well as the variously designed stucco areas of the balustrades. Design adaptations to contemporary developments were obviously seen as desireable.

15 Schneider und Schmelzer, *Industriearchitektur im Wandel der Zeit* (see note 5), p. 25.

16 A no less instructive integration of external steel supports—without however cladding them—was achieved twenty years later by Hans Döllgast in Munich. Here, with the rebuilding of the Alte Pinakothek, the first measure undertaken was a protective roof with supports. As with Manz, the load-bearing rounded steel supports are set in the existing axial spacing and slightly outside of the edges of the building, so that the reconstruction could also proceed via dry construction. The filigree, unclad, flat rounded supports—given the inconspicuous appearance of rooftop water pipes—rhythmicize the simplified, restored façade section and assume, in a way similar to Manz's colossal order, the function of the now lost pilasters.

17 Goethe's descriptions of the Palazzo della Ragione, also known as the Basilica Palladiana, which was renovated and expanded according to plans by Andrea Palladio between 1549 and 1614, are found in the entry dated Vicenza, September 19, in Johann Wolfgang Goethe, *Italian Journey,* trans. E. H. Auden and Elizabeth Mayer (London: 1962), pp. 63–64.

18 Ibid.

COMPOUNDING OF EPOCHS

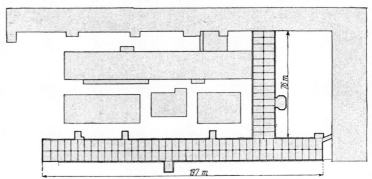

1 Construction site photograph, 1927. Visible on the right is the mobile crane runway for the serial erection of the prefabricated steel trusses.
2 The Salamander Shoe Factory in Kornwestheim, circa 1920. The management was accommodated in the head building at the street crossing; adjoining it on the left and parallel to the track system is the so-called Hundred Meter Building prior to its vertical extension.
3 Situation plan of the vertical extension of the so-called Hundred Meter Building (197 meters in length) and the adjoining orthogonal courtyard wing (76 meters in length).

4 The vertical extension as a steel skeleton with external load transfer (right) and its cladding by means of brickwork (left).

5 View of the east façade: the Hundred Meter Building after completion of the vertical extension, raising it from three to five stories.

COMPOUNDING OF EPOCHS

ENGINEERING COMMENTARY
DANIEL MEYER AND
PATRIC FISCHLI-BOSON

Since the additional loading of the façade walls and supports is not an option, the vertical extension, executed in steel construction, is decoupled from the existing support structure by means of an exoskeleton. The ceiling loads at the center of the building are suspended by means of ties to the truss girders above. The so-called king post truss is formed as a triangular lattice and spans the entire building width, 15 meters, with a structural height of 3.4 meters. The trusses lie on the façade, whose setback measures 0.45 meters, on dispersed compression members—the so-called Vierendeel trusses—in a straddle mounting. The supports, composed of angle profiles and flat bars, in turn lie on the cross beams of the ceiling above the third upper story. The crossbeams span the existing façade walls and discharge the loads via the external supports into the punctually strengthened foundation. In order to minimize buckling legs, the 12-meter-long supports are fixed at 1/3 and 2/3 points of the existing façade structure. The stiffening of the building in the longitudinal and transverse directions is achieved primarily via the roof membrane, which transfer the forces into the staircases that are situated at regular intervals. The longitudinal stiffening is additionally secured via the masonry façade. The long façade forms a continuous system of supports and beams with flexurally rigid corners.

COMPOUNDING OF EPOCHS

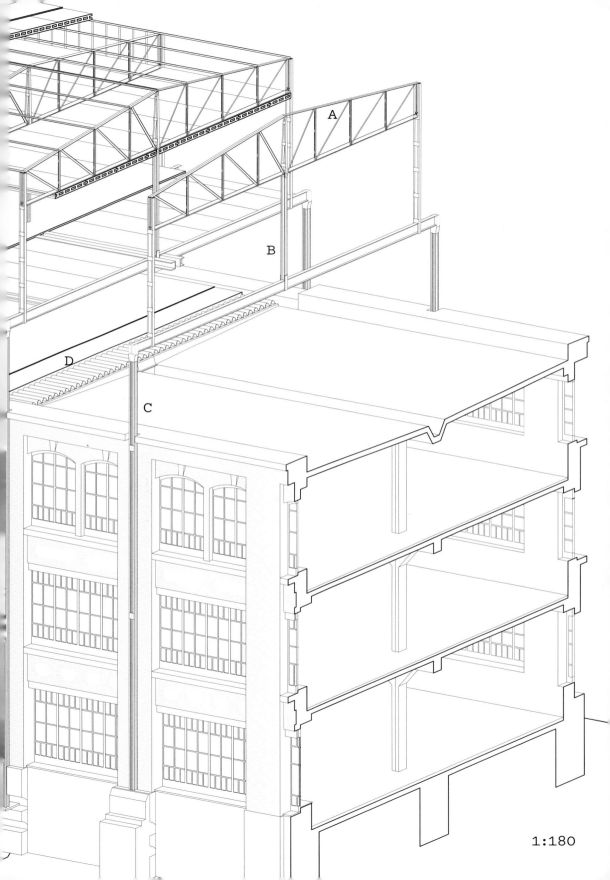

PROCESSES OF REPLACEMENT

Constructing Vertical Extensions— Reassessing Italian Postwar Modernism

Matteo Iannello   p. 52

Design through Constructive Thinking: The Extension of the Faculty of Architecture in Hannover by Friedrich Spengelin and Horst Wunderlich (1961–1966)

Daniel Stockhammer   p. 64

PROCESSES OF REPLACEMENT

1

2

3

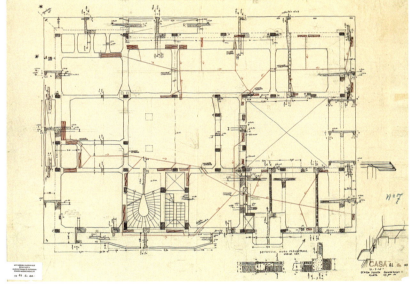

The original building becomes a post office: vertical
extension of the Villino Allatri in Rome, 1949–1952, by
Mario Ridolfi, Wolfgang Frankl, and Mario Fiorentino.

PROCESSES OF REPLACEMENT   54

Constructing Vertical Extensions— Reassessing Italian Postwar Modernism

Matteo Iannello

Initiated by the landing of English and American troops on the southeastern coast of Sicily during the night of July 9/10, 1943, the successive occupation of the peninsula began; it was followed by an extended armed conflict in which two armies confronted one another in a war of liberation that ended only in April of 1945. Heavy fighting and allied bombardment across the entire peninsula from north to south left its mark on the territory. After the war, reconstruction work represented a priority for the new government, and moreover on two fronts: first, with regard to the "housing question," i. e. the urgent need for new living space, and secondly with economic and productive revitalization through the resumption of and support for industrial productivity.

At the same time, the reconstruction of the region opened up the possibility of converting into future resources everything the war had obliterated so dramatically: "I wander through the ruins of Milan. Why do I experience such enthusiasm? I really should be sad, but instead, I tingle with joy. […] Vivid ideas strike my mind like the breath of the purest and most radiant morning. I can feel that out of this death, a new life is rising, that from these ruins, a stronger, richer, more beautiful city will rise."[1]

Savinio's words convey the significance of the drama he had lived through; even stronger however was the hope for rebirth, for a different future, one that would have to be conceptualized and recorded in a new language. In particular for architecture, it was a question of a perspective shared by an almost completely "new" generation of architects and engineers. They were determined to win back lost terrain, to experiment, to implement a new and powerful form of linguistic expression. Generally speaking, these were the same topics addressed in 1951 at the eighth CIAM Congress (Congrès Internationaux d'Architecture Moderne), and which was first synthesized in Ernesto Nathan Roger's report, as well as in the subsequent publication *Il cuore della città*.[2] They testify to specifically Italian traits within a debate that involved the most important European architects.

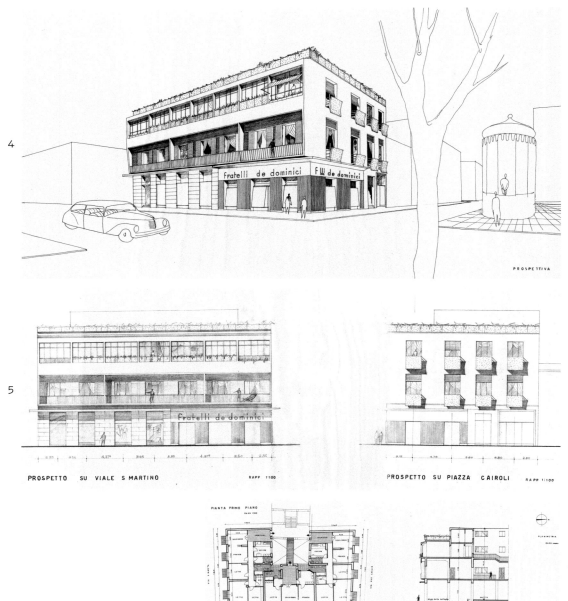

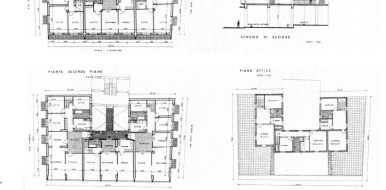

Strengthening the existent by means of vertical extension: the Celi Building on Viale San Martino in Messina, 1949–1950, by Roberto Calandra and Pasquale Marino.

PROCESSES OF REPLACEMENT

Given the dense and strongly artistic *tessuto* [fabric] of Italy's cities, new residential projects had to be installed at peripheral locations. They were co-ordinated by means of successive development plans, and were for the most part bound up with subsidized construction (Ina Casa, Gescal, etc.).[3] Within the urban texture of these historic cities themselves, in contrast, action was based upon fine adjustments and selective interventions (restoration, reno-vation, replacement, …). Emerging from such renovation, revitalization, and conversion efforts for residential buildings were some interesting themes, for the new architecture entered into dialogue with historical material. Through a confrontation not just at the level of expression, but on those of technics and technology as well, a project might often achieve greater quantitative and qualitative value than the predecessor structure.

This is true as well for the three projects selected for the present es-say: three case studies consisting of two residential buildings in Rome and Messina, as well as an office building in Milan. In each instance, the inter-vention generated an addition that followed historically established prac-tice, adapted however in the grammar of a new language and in a way that opened up an urgent dialogue with the existing architectural substance. Each intervention unfolded its full expressive force, obviously offset from the pre-existent structure, through a refusal—which is also evident in the new mate-rials and technologies used—of any purely linguistic imitation.

The vertical extension of the Villino ("Little Villa") Allatri on Via Paisiello in Rome—which was carried out in 1949–1952 by Mario Ridolfi, Wolfgang Frankl, and Mario Fiorentino—is the first in this series of case studies. The original structure, a residential building built in 1928 by Ballio Morpurgo, is interpreted here almost exclusively as a pedestal for the new intervention: "On top of a two-story building, done in a neo-baroque style so sugary it can almost be regarded as a blank space, as a negative, the ar-chitects have placed a new three-story volume. The question arose now of whether this pedestal, upon which the new construction rests, was to have been incorporated as an integral component—at the very least as contributing a rhythm—or whether it was to have remained a simple support, a base, a neutral foundation. This problematic, which could also have been reversed as a negative, functioned as a kind of stimulus for the architects. Arguably, they worked coherently on the basis of the old structure, but also succeeded in focusing attention on the new, the superstructure."[4] While the new super-structure on top of the existing building, which was "handled almost like an empty fact of nature,"[5] seemed to allow no leeway for formal concessions to Ballio Morpurgo's highly controversial Roman neo-baroque style, the mod-ern superstructure constructed a new architectural image in which old and new participate to an equal degree. One could even assert that the superstruc-ture draws its form from the rich heritage of baroque expression, while at the same time modifying and translating it into new forms and concepts.

The existing masonry structure was used, then, as the substructure and foundation for the extension, consisting of reinforced concrete: a C-shaped

57

layout was inscribed in a space framework which projects beyond the lower cuboid, and which is characterized by the horizontal rhythm of the stories, with their long, continuous, projecting balconies.[6] In the ground plan, the arrangement of the interior spaces and the perspectival sequence of transitions and views are organized by the orthogonal arrangement of transparent partition walls and a sophisticated compositional and structural design. The contrasting articulation of the three levels (in the transition from the private interiors to the common areas, and all the way to the conservatories and the terraces) corresponds to an equally diverse structure in section and elevation. The composition—executed on the outside with plastered masonry web bracing—is characterized by the varied design of the balustrades, which in some cases are given an almost sculptural effect through the insertion of concrete flowerpots: profiles and textured glass on the first and second levels, railings of metal stakes on the top story.

The series of numerous design drawings and studies,[7] on which the various handwritings of the architects alternate and are superimposed, on the one hand reflect the genuine project-related construction and the compositional search which is bound up with the architectural design. On the other (in the often highly realistic drawings of construction details and their installation), they highlight work on the definition of all of the components, including the selection of materials and colors, windows and doors, as well as the differentiation of surfaces.

Although they adopt a number of traits from the existing building (the symmetry of the façade toward the Via Bellina and the repetition of the corner solution with loggia), Ridolfi, Frankl, and Fiorentino display a new approach to creating architecture: it is not just a question of solving or shaping an architectural problem, but at the same time of working on the urban character of the project, whose volume is positioned in its complexity as the "pivot at the crossing of its four streets."[8]

Analogous considerations, albeit in a completely different local context, come into play with the reconstruction and vertical extension of the Celi Building on Viale San Martino in Messina by Roberto Calandra[9] and Pasquale Marino (realized 1949–1950).

After a major earthquake that occurred on December 28, 1908,[10] the town on the Strait of Messina was completely reconstructed in accordance with special requirements and with the help of new planning instruments. Since precise ordinances regulating the construction of new tall buildings in an extremely earthquake-prone area were lacking, realization proceeded step-by-step via adaptation to the intended building heights. This modus operandi continued until 1959 when, in the wake of the Convegno Internazionale di Ingegneria Sismica, which met in Messina and was organized by Calandra, a new set of standards was adopted. The design for the Celi building slipped through the existing legal loophole. It envisions a vertical extension of two additional stories plus a new top floor, to be saddled onto the existing building. Although the character and architectural quality of the existing building differs markedly from Morpurgo's residential building, Calandra's approach is identical to that of Ridolfi, Frankl, and Fiorentino. Here, a new structure in reinforced concrete is set on top of a concrete substructure, which is additionally strengthened by the measures undertaken: a simple framework carries the upper three levels, which are arranged into a C-shaped layout, each with three apartment units. In elevation, a continuous awning between the ground floor and the first upper story emphasizes the transition between commercial uses in the pedestal volume and the apartments, which are distributed within the upper levels. The latter are brought together in a frame structure that concentrates and accentuates the unity of the architectural mass. The result is a façade layout that is completed by the system of a double loggia toward the street front (open in the first upper story, with a long balcony; characterized in the second upper story by the rhythm of the large windows), while the lateral façades display small projecting balconies consisting of bush-hammered concrete at regular intervals. To be sure, it is still a question here of an embryonic approach in the pre-project stage, which would have been enriched during the phases of implementation planning and realization by a series of high-quality solutions, and hence would have followed the established practice that consistently characterized Calandra's works.

Given their characteristics and their diversity, the cases investigated here represent two typical instances of a modus operandi that was widespread in Italian postwar architecture, and which was bound up with the relationship between old and new. These examples should therefore be considered within a far broader picture, one that needless to say also includes vertical extension projects whose dimensions are far more modest than those of the original structure, particularly in the Milanese context.[11]

This pertains as well, finally, to the last example in this brief overview: a design related not to the theme of housing, and instead to the far less codified and in a number of respects experimental realm of industrial architecture. Between 1951 and 1957, commissioned by the firm of Loro e Parisini, which specialized in construction machinery, Luigi Caccia Dominioni[12] designed and realized the extension of the factory, which involved the incorporation and vertical extension of part of the original structures: "The designer's core idea was to position a very long 'command bridge' above the existing buildings, so that the lower part could remain intact in its main features, while giving the offices maximal visibility."[13] After a number of rejected approaches,[14] the intervention was concretized as the construction of a unified and cohesive block along Via Savona which terminates on one side with the rectangular volume of the cafeteria, and on the other, facing the Via Brunelleschi, with a projecting building section designed to serve management and to contain conference rooms, and which underscores the idea of a floating "bridge."

Caccia Dominioni realized a compact block that is spatially articulated in section with a long front measuring 150 meters above the existing ground story, which is clad entirely in hexagonal clinker slabs. This level was formulated as a rigid masonry pedestal, and is broken only at the entrance,

Reshaping and reinterpretation: factory expansion for Loro e Parisini on Via Savona in Milan, 1951–1957, by Luigi Caccia Dominioni.

PROCESSES OF REPLACEMENT

above which a large drafting room seems to float. The pedestal, which appears from the outside as a closed, compact structural element, contrasts with the transparency of the new "command bridge." Defining the appearance of the entire street front is the elegant rhythm of its glazing, consisting of dark-gray anodized aluminum, and characterized by alternating fixed and movable elements, as well as by the distinction between the types of glass utilized (insulating and cathedral glass). Running in front of it is the elevated metal bridge, which unites "decorative and functional features."[15]

Unlike the designs by Ridolfi, Frankl, and Fiorentino for the Villino Allatri in Rome and by Calandra for the Celi Building in Messina, wherein the vertical extensions are conceived as pure reinforced concrete structures, the extension developed by Caccia Dominioni is executed in lightweight construction: a structure in steel profiles and clear and structured glass, whose lightness is emphasized by the Eternit saddle roof which covers the entire longitudinal volume. Here, steel construction made possible optimal solutions for various interior utilization demands, facilitating access and generating maximal flexibility for the organization and allocation of surface areas. Running longitudinally through the "command bridge" in the upper story is a long corridor. The firm's offices—structured through a lightweight, opaque partition-wall system, and given skylights in structured glass—are arranged on either side. Deployed in order to attain greater flexibility regarding the distribution of the offices are mobile, modular walls with expansive glazing, which at the same time guarantee ideal light distribution in these spaces. Inserted with the same intention is the continuous, 8-meter-tall Primalith glass-brick wall, which delimits the anteroom of the staircase that leads to the offices.

Caccia devoted special attention to the technical and technological aspects of the project; and he determined the installations, the choice of applied materials (steel, concrete, transparent and structured glass, rubber, wood), and the various surface treatments in dependency upon natural systems. In this sense, the lightweight construction with steel frames and continuous glazing, which shapes the view of the entire office volume along the Via Savona, essentially defines an installation wall that amalgamates neon lighting, sun-shades, as well as heating and cooling elements in all interior spaces.

The design for the Loro e Parisini factory expansion involves many of the themes that characterized Caccia's work over a period of many years: cladding, façade layout, design, and the precise definition of details. These are aspects that are already present in the work of Ridolfi, and which were developed further by Calandra, albeit in a different manner, and needless to say with different results. The three case studies investigated here, although they—unavoidably—provide only a partial view of the multiform and complex panorama of Italian postwar architecture, encompass *in nuce* many of the problems that characterize the work of an entire generation of architects who oscillated between tradition and modernism, between investigations of the new and judicious readings of the past.

10

11

Interior circulation in the factory
expansion for Loro e Parisini by Luigi
Caccia Dominioni.

1   Alberto Savinio, *Ascolta il tuo cuore,* 1st ed. 1944 (Milan: 1992), p. 396.
2   Ernesto Nathan Rogers, Josep Lluís Sert and Jaqueline Tyrwhitt (eds.), *Il cuore della città: per una vita più umana della comunità* (Milan: 1954).
3   Among the important publications on these projects are: Luigi Beretta Anguissola (ed.), *I quattordici anni del piano Ina Casa* (Rome: 1963); and Paola Di Biagi, *La grande ricostruzione: il piano INA Casa e l'Italia degli anni Cinquanta* (Rome: 2001).
4   "Una sopraelevazione a Roma," in *Metron,* 51 (1954), p. 27.
5   Francesco Cellini, Claudio D'Amato, *Le architetture di Ridolfi e Frankl* (Milan: 2005), p. 53.
6   "The new typological order"—according to Mario Fiorentino—"has its origin and model in the C-shaped layout of Casa Colombo, 1936, built by Ridolfi in S. Valentino. In this way, a layout developed for a specific solution has become a repeatable typological element." Mario Fiorentino, *La casa: Progetti 1946–1981* (Rome: 1985), p. 40.
7   The Ridolfi-Frankl-Malagricci Archive, preserved in the Accademia Nazionale di San Luca, contains eighty-two project drawings for the vertical extension of the Villino Allatri and nineteen photographs of the finished building.
8   Fiorentino, *La casa* (see note 6), p. 40.
9   Born in Messina November 2, 1915, Calandra moved to Rome with his family in 1930, where he studied architecture and earned a Diploma degree in 1937. This was followed in 1939 by a Master of Science in Architecture from Columbia University in New York. As a founding member of the APAO, he worked among others with Carlo Scarpa and Giuseppe Samonà. Calandra died in Palermo in 2015. See Matteo Iannello, "Roberto Calandra architetto e maieuta," in Massimilano Marafon Pecoraro and Pierfrancesco Palazzotto (eds.), *Archivi di Architettura a Palermo. Memorie della città (XVII–XX secolo)* (Caltanissetta: 2012), pp. 120–131.
10 See Paola Barbera, "Messina después del terremoto del 1908: nuévas técnicas y lenguajes antiguos," in *Actas del Noveno Congreso Nacional y Primer Congreso Internacional Hispano-americano de Historia de la construcctiòn* (Segovia: 2015), vol. 1, pp. 177–187
11 See, in particular, the vertical extension of the Villa Pestarini by Franco Albini (1949) and the designs of the BBPR partnership for buildings on the Porta Vercellina (1955) and for the Banca Privata Finanziaria on Via Verdi (1966). Other examples are the conversion and vertical extension of the Villino Astaldi, executed by Mario Ridolfi in Rome (1955–1956), and Gino Becker's vertical extension on Via Baretti in Turin (1958). Another project, albeit with a deliberately provocative character and on a different scale, is the proposal by Superstudio for a superstructure on top of the Colosseum in Rome (1969).
12 In collaboration with the construction engineer Vittorio Dubini. See "Il 'Securit' nell'architettura," in *Domus,* 330 (1957), pp. 49–51; "Fabbricato per Uffici," in *Edilizia Moderna,* 62 (1957), pp. 9–18; "Fabbricato per Uffici," in *Vitrum,* 95 (1957), pp. 2–13; "I nuovi edifici di uno stabilimento a Milano," in *Casabella Continuità,* 217, 4, (1957), pp. 42–47; "Luigi Caccia Dominioni," in *Werk, Bauen + Wohnen,* 12 (2013) (monographic volume).
13 "I nuovi edifici …" (see note 12), p. 43.
14 "At an earlier point in time, a building with a vertical development was designed that was to have been erected above the old building, but ultimately, the concept was implemented as a horizontal volume." "Fabbricato per Uffici," (see note 12), p. 3.
15 Ibid., p. 4.

PROCESSES OF REPLACEMENT

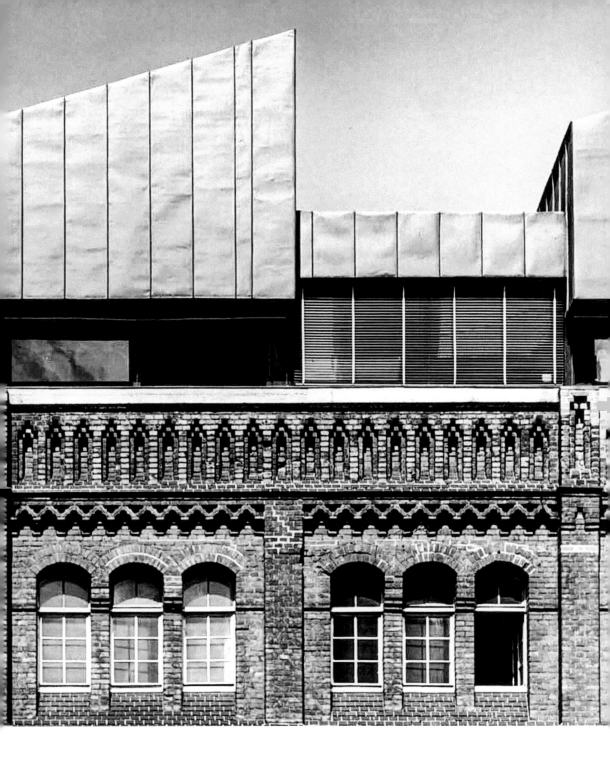

Design through Constructive Thinking

The Extension of the Faculty of Architecture in Hannover by Friedrich Spengelin and Horst Wunderlich (1961–1966)
Daniel Stockhammer

Examining the era of European reconstruction, vertical extensions constitute a special case. Between restoration and new building, the new postwar Germany, in particular, offered a broad test field for concepts of "building in existing contexts";[1] vertical extensions, however, remained the exception. A relationship of tension between preservation and replacement, between the demands of conservation and modern postulates, is therefore already inherent in the task. A constructive and historical examination of a hitherto largely unknown project demonstrates that it is possible to successfully bridge these antagonistic ideologies.

DEMOLITION AS PROTECTIVE MEASURE

During the night of February 10/11, 1941, when British military aircraft mounted the first large-scale attack on the so-called Oststadt in Hannover, individual strikes inflicted damage all the way to the south of the Welfengarten—the premises of the Technical University.[2] Here, directly at Horst-Wessel-Platz (today Königsworther Platz), the explosion destroyed the upper two stories of the main section of the building of Hannover's School of Architecture. Blast waves broke away middle sections and corner turrets up to

the second uppermost story, shattering windowpanes, while down to the middle story, window frames were blown out from the inside (fig. 2).[3]

Only four years earlier, the Federal State of Lower Saxony had purchased a building belonging to the large-scale printing establishment of König & Ebhard for the expansion of its Technical University.[4] With five stories on Nienburger Strasse and three stories at right angles to them along Schlosswender Strasse, the L-shaped structure formed the upbeat to the industrial complex that meandered along the street (fig. 1). The complex had been designed in stages by the architect Heinrich G. L. Frühling (1833–1906) between 1874 and 1893; as an exponent of the Hannover School of Architecture, Frühling clad the buildings in historicist brick façades, mainly in neo-Gothic style (fig. 3).[5] The sale of portions of the complex in 1937 proved a godsend for the school (today the Leibniz Universität Hannover); it soon made extensive, flexibly divisible surfaces available for architectural instruction in immediate proximity to the university.[6]

During and immediately after World War II, there was no possibility of rebuilding or even restoring damaged parts of the building. A simple emergency roof was erected to protect the open ruins, and the building shell sealed again as far as possible.[7] Demolished at the same time were the heavily damaged upper stories of the head section of the building up to the intact height of the façade—the lower edges of the windowsills of the third upper story. The remaining openings beneath this caesura, including truncated window openings and broken segments of masonry,[8] were bricked up using old rubble (ref. 1, fig. 5). The resultant "cutting plane" made possible the horizontal production of a simple, shallow-sloped emergency roof, while however allowing the height of the original head section of the building to remain lower than that of its elongated prolongation.

Evidently, the building owes its survival to the pragmatism of this "wartime amputation"; without these consolidation measures—and in times of such acute material shortage—the destruction of the original substance by weathering influences would probably have been unavoidable. Moreover, simple repair measures facilitated the rapid resumption of teaching activity, and transformed the former factory building into a memorial of German pre- and postwar history.[9]

FINALIZING THE FORM

By the 1950s, a rapidly rising student population and a growing shortage of workspaces made an expansion of the architecture department indispensable; in the 1970s, plans for the School's expansion envisioned a new building. Urgency and limited financial resources shifted attention toward a vertical extension as a cost-saving alternative, for the principle of a "prosthesis" promised to be advantageous in a number of respects:

– urbanistic enhancement through a new volume in conformity with historical models;

– the cost-free replacement of the emergency protective roof from the war;
– the organizational advantages of retaining the existing substance and new functions within the same building; and
– continuing operations during the building phase.

In 1961, as a touchstone of quality, so to speak, the task was assigned to the architect Friedrich Spengelin (1925–2016), who had just been appointed to a professorship at the school, along with his assistant Horst Wunderlich.

As a student of Hans Döllgast,[10] Spengelin was presumably familiar early on with the theme of reconstruction and with the "creative preservation of historic monuments"—the reinterpretation and modification of a pre-existing architectural inventory.[11] Spengelin had earned his Diploma degree in 1948 at the Technische Hochschule in Munich before working for Konstanty Gutschow, the "architect of the redesign of the Hanseatic City of Hamburg" and the co-author of the work *Umbau* [conversion].[12] After the war, Gutschow also drew up an urbanistic concept for Hannover, which hence also encompassed Spengelin's planning work at Königsworther Platz.[13] Spengelin's urbanistic response now followed the specifications of his teacher,[14] in that he restored the building's original volume and its function as an upbeat to Schlosswender Strasse: a closed monolith as a new "main section" in place of the destroyed upper stories at the street crossing, and the shed-style design of the roof structures lying crosswise in relation to the longitudinal building in place of the old emergency roof. He understood the completion of the building as being analogous to the anthropomorphic articulation of feet, torso, and head: the building "[…] should have a head [...], which clearly represents the culmination of the 'body.'" The tripartite structure that had been lost in the war would now be restored in the language of modernism.

According to Rudolf Hillebrecht, Hannover's master architect (and also a student of Gutschow), there would in any event have been too little original substance for a precise historical reconstruction. "Today, with buildings in a similar condition, well-intentioned people would certainly raise the question of whether—[assuming] the availability of the requisite technical skill in brick building—the missing sections should be supplemented,"[15] to cite the architect himself. They should, however, be interested exclusively in "modern solutions,"[16] which is why they ought to have opted—through a commitment to the new ideals—for a visible separation from the pre-existing structure by means of powerful joints. For after the war, according to Hannover's master architect, it was a question not of reconstructing pre-existing substance, but instead of "preserving, strengthening, or adding to its essential traits" which are determinative "for its individual character."[17] (fig. 4).

CONSTRUCTION AND THE REFORMATION OF THE DESIGN

Work on the vertical elevation began with the raising of the lower-lying roof edge of the existing building to the height of the adjacent longitudinal wing. Using brick (presumably rubble), the war-damaged parts of the building up to the upper edge of the existing dwarf gallery were repaired (ref. 2, fig. 5). This unified roof-edge height of the old building was now defined as the new parapet height and windowsills, a powerful cornice of the first added story. As a glazed seam, a continuous ribbon window above it divides the original building optically from the new roof structures.

The vertical extension of the head section of the building—which consisted now of three of its original five stories—was carried out without additional strengthening of the existing support structure. The load-bearing portions of the first additional story and the new suspended ceiling were carried out in solid construction; the outside walls were supported by a timber framework (square timbers measuring 80×80 millimeters) and to some extent walled from behind with "half-block lightweight construction walls."[18] Non-load-bearing partition walls were executed in wood and wood-and-metal construction.

The masterpiece is the structural concept for the vertical extension of the elongated building, whose interior support structure, consisting of cast-iron supports, could not accept additional loads. A steel girder grid (A on the axonometry)—carried by the existing external walls—forms the replacement ceiling of the old emergency roof and the floor of the first added story. Additional loads could be absorbed by the new floor across a span of 16 meters, because it was suspended in the middle section from steel girders (presumably plate girders) (C) via tie rods (B). These girders in turn rest on the supports at those points on the outer walls that manifest the greatest resisting force: the points of intersection between the outer façade and its pilasters. The axial dimension of the supports and girders, which also follow the interior division of the space, therefore correspond to the articulation of the façade. The ribbon window of the first added story encloses the bearing supports and follows their rhythm with its window divisions. Frame extensions conceal the supports set behind them. Linked together in pairs, four pairs of supports are formed from the eight load-bearing steel girders. A secondary construction in corrugated web beams (D)[19]—presumably timber frameworks and a planking that connects the ceiling, wall, and floor surfaces by means of rough-sawn spruce planks (E)—stiffens and encloses the pairs of supports to form space-containing supporting structures.[20]

As a result of a structural and constructive concept, therefore, the supporting structures allows the historic façade to remain perceptible, using contemporary resources to achieve a reformation of the structure. With their northeastern orientation, the monopitch roofs of the superstructures, which recall the typology of the shed roofs of manufacturing plants (fig. on title page), facilitate optimal illumination in the workrooms (fig. 6).[21] Via staircases, each of these space frameworks—planned as drafting halls for architecture students—is linked to workrooms lying across from one another in the story below. As in a gallery, this results in view axes between the workrooms and the superstructures above (fig. 7). A central corridor, lit naturally by skylights, serves as the main access to the workrooms. The wood construction, which serves to stiffen the steel components, acts simultaneously as cladding and as room surfaces. The panel cladding, which makes a rustic impression, is untreated.

Necessary in order to adhere to the tight budget was the economical handling and precise application of materials and construction in all parts of the building. The horizontal roof surfaces (which have gradients of 1 percent), for example, consists only of bituminous sheeting. An additional shingle roofing would have meant more weight, and hence a more costly support structure. Only inclined and upright façade surfaces—i. e. those visible from the outside—are clad in copper sheeting. Additional measures such as the parsimonious use of thermal insulation and single glazing (meanwhile replaced) allowed weight and hence costs to be reduced even further.

Even taking into account the sacrifice of certain conveniences, and adjusted for inflation, the building costs of somewhat more than 1 million German marks were extraordinarily low. In his inaugural speech, the rector emphasized the minimal expenditure as a particularly praiseworthy achievement by the architect.[22] When it comes to generating atmosphere with little money, much can be learned from Spengelin's vertical extension—at least from the perspective of one contemporary: "Assuming it is even possible to speak about models when it comes to architectural production […], then this building points to the fact that even today, with the enormous offerings from the building and supply industry, economical building remains appealing and sensible,"[23] we read in a text marking the thirtieth anniversary of the extension.

Not in the form of overt display, but instead through its precise application and in conjunction with other materials, Spengelin was able to exploit the performance capacities of steel in an optimal way. The extension in Hannover demonstrates that the painstaking analysis of existing framework conditions, and a construction type and choice of materials that respond to it with precision, can lead to an immanent connection between old and new. Not merely the architect's creative drive, but postwar cost-cutting pressures along with material shortages compelled the retelling of an old story in the language of a new era. Spengelin's and Wunderlich's extension from 1966 is not a restoration, but instead the reformation of an old form.

6 Wolfgang Pietsch: "Von der Grossdruckerei zum Hochschulbereich. Erwerb und Umnutzung des Grundstücks der Druckerei König & Ebhardt, Schlosswender Strasse 5," in Sid Auffarth and Wolfgang Pietsch (eds.), *Die Universität Hannover. Ihre Bauten. Ihre Gärten. Ihre Planungsgeschichte* (Petersberg: 2003), pp. 247–250, here p. 247.

7 Exactly when professional preservation measures were begun remains unclear. Since the building suffered damage relatively early in the war, immediate protective measures are conceivable. The other damaged facilities were almost completely demolished after the war.

8 See also in the illustrations the truncated openings of the former pointed arched windows above the main entrance on the southeastern side of the head of the building.

9 See Paulhans Peters, "Not und Tugend. Das Architekturgebäude der Universität Hannover von Friedrich Spengelin und Horst Wunderlich, 1964–1966," in *Deutsche Bauzeitung db,* 5, no. 130 (1996), pp. 100–105, here p. 101.

10 Hans Döllgast (1891–1974) is regarded as one of the most important architects of German reconstruction. With buildings such as the Alte Pinakothek in Munich, he contributed substantially to the establishment of the so-called creative preservation of monuments.

11 Cf. "Kunst nach 1945," in Alois Schmid (ed.), *Handbuch der Bayerischen Geschichte,* vol. 4, 2nd sub-volume, 2nd revised edition (Munich: 2007; 1st edition, Munich: 1975), p. 675.

12 Konstanty Gutschow and Hermann Zippel, *Umbau: Fassadenveränderung, Ladeneinbau, Wohnhausumbau, Wohnungsteilung, seitliche Erweiterung, Aufstockung, Zweckveränderung. Planung und Konstruktion. 86 Beispiele mit 392 vergleichenden Ansichten, Grundrissen und Schnitten* (Stuttgart: 1932).

13 See Konstanty Gutschow, *Stadtmitte Hannover. Beiträge zur Aufbauplanung der Innenstadt* (Hannover: 1949). In light of denazification efforts in Germany, Gutschow was barred from a leading or official position in postwar planning.

14 See "Aufbauplan Innenstadt Hannover," prepared by the architect Konstanty Gutschow, dated September 20, 1949, in: ibid., no pag. (appendix).

15 Friedrich Spengelin, "Alt und Neu. Bauen im historischen Kontext: Die Aufstockung des Gebäudes der Architekturabteilung und der Umbau der Marstallruine als Teil der Universitätsbibliothek," in Auffarth and Pietsch *(see note 6)*, p. 252.

16 Spengelin refers here to models such as Gunnar Asplund's modern extension of the town hall in Gothenborg. Ibid., p. 253.

17 Rudolf Hillebrecht, "Zum Wiederaufbau nach 1945," in: Architektenkammer Niedersachsen (ed.), *Architektur in Hannover seit 1900* (Munich: 1981), p. 12.

18 See Peters, "Not und Tugend" (see note 9), pp. 102–103.

19 Corrugated web beams are characteristic of economical building in postwar Europe: they have a double T-section with wooden flanges and a plywood web that is press-fitted and glued into wave-shaped grooves on the inner side of the flanges. The waveform gives the extremely thin flange its stiffness to prevent buckling.

20 The principle of the space-containing support structure would have been familiar to Spengelin, at the latest with Alejandro de la Sota's gymnasium for the Colegio Maravillas in Madrid. It was completed and published in 1962, which coincides with the design phase of Spengelin's extension.

21 See also the architect's report in: Friedrich Spengelin, "Aufstockung des Architekturgebäudes der TU Hannover: Druckerei – Ruine – Architekturabteilung," in *Baumeister,* 65, no. 9 (1968), pp. 1008–1011.

22 See also: Friedrich Spengelin, *Alt und Neu: Bauen im historischen Kontext* (see note 15), p. 254.

23 Peters, "Not und Tugend" (see note 9), p. 105.

1 For example the reinterpretation of historical models (e. g., Joseph Schwarz, Schloss Johannisberg in Rheingau, 1943–1951), "critical reconstruction" (e. g., Hans Döllgast, Alte Pinakothek, Munich, 1946–1957) or "creative" extension (e. g., Dominikus and Gottfried Böhm, Liebfrauenkirche, Püttlingen, 1953–1954).

2 Friedrich Spengelin, the architect of the vertical extension, repeatedly mentions 1943 as the year of destruction. Data derived from photos from the end of the war and a report from the Allies concerning bombing raids by the Royal Air Force in Hannover suggest that the building was destroyed earlier, in 1941. See "10./11.02.1941 RAF 204t," in Hannover Field Report, USSBS, 1947—appendix B; cited from www.mast-forum.de, (last accessed July 1, 2016).

3 Information drawn from image materials of the war-damaged building, photos from February 10/11, 1941, author unknown (Stadtarchiv Hannover).

4 Also a story related by a student at the architecture department of the TH Hannover about the period before the war, in Friedrich Lindau, *Architektur und Stadt: Erinnerungen eines neunzigjährigen hannoverschen Architekten* (Lamspringe: 2005), pp. 88–94.

5 Erected almost at the same time was a "sister building" for the Benecke & Schwarz oilcloth factory in Hannover-Vinnhorst; it remained for the most part spared by the war and was later also given a vertical extension.

1

1 The large-scale printing establishment of König & Ebhard Hannover (1895) with the head section of the building at the corner of Nienburger Strasse and Schlosswender Strasse, by the architect Heinrich G. L. Frühling.

PROCESSES OF REPLACEMENT

3

4

2 The head section of the building immediately after partial destruction in 1941.
3 View of Königsworther Platz (then Horst Wessel Platz), circa 1930.
4 View from Königsworther Platz, circa 1990.

PROCESSES OF REPLACEMENT 74

5 The concept of "repair work": makeshift filling at the end of the war by means of rubble (1) and simplified partial reconstruction (2) through the leveling of the new balustrade edge.

6   Interior view after completion: drafting hall in the gallery.
7   View from the first added story into the gallery above.

PROCESSES OF REPLACEMENT

ENGINEERING COMMENTARY
DANIEL MEYER AND
PATRIC FISCHLI-BOSON

The one-story superstructure plus gallery traverses the building in a crosswise direction, and has a span of 16.7 meters. The load is transferred to the façade walls via the main girders and steel supports. The ceiling above the third upper story is attached to the main girders from below via tension elements, so that this ceiling delivers no additional loads to the cast-iron inner supports. The construction of the main girders cannot be determined on the basis of the available planning documents. Conceivable are lattice girders, rolled steel joists, or welded plate girders. Given the span width and the limited structural height, welded plate girders seem probable. Likewise, the position of the window bars, which transfer the loads from the roof onto the supports, and the tension elements of the ceiling suspension are not congruent. With a lattice girder, this would have resulted in the bending of the tension and compression flanges. For these reasons, we assume welded plate girders were used. This would indeed have been a typical construction method for the 1960s. Horizontal reinforcement was achieved by the staircase in the head section of the building, as well as by the staircase in the appended extension.

PROCESSES OF REPLACEMENT

1:165

TECHNOLOGICAL EUPHORIA

The Psychology of the High-Flyer—On the Vertical Extension of Vienna since Deconstructivism

Lorenzo De Chiffre   p. 82

Taming the Future in the Tube: The Design for the Extension of the Kunstakademie Düsseldorf by Karl Wimmenauer, Lyubo-Mir Szabo, and Ernst Kasper in 1968

Martin Tschanz   p. 94

TECHNOLOGICAL EUPHORIA 82

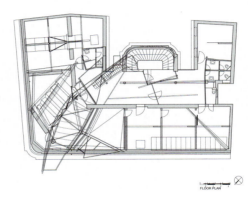
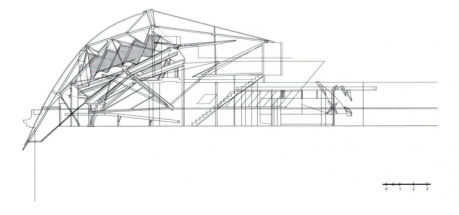

Coop Himmelb(l)au, rooftop extension, Falkestrasse, 1988. Classified in building regulation terms partly as art-in-architecture and partly as a roofed terrace, the structure rests on the approximately 8-centimeter-thin length of the old brick walls. As the first work by the freshly graduated project-architect Franz Sam, the complex geometry of this non-concentric steel structure was calculated with the aid of a piece of self-written computer software.
Structural-framework planning: Oskar Graf

TECHNOLOGICAL EUPHORIA 84

The Psychology of the High-Flyer—On the Vertical Extension of Vienna since Deconstructivism

Lorenzo De Chiffre

Above and beyond conventional urban renewal, the numerous rooftop extensions promoted by the Vienna municipal authorities as a form of urban post-densification can in fact be seen as an inner urban expansion. Vienna is—akin to Paris and Berlin—the epitome of a vertical European metropolis. London, by contrast, can be referred to as the paradigm of a horizontally spread-out city.[1] This elementary distinction is evident, amongst other features, in the respective types of post-densification and their direct relationship to the predominant housing form: the tenement blocks of the *Gründerzeit* era in the one case, and the terraced house in the other. In this sense, one of the most common forms of expansion of private living space in London is the so-called backyard extension, which expands horizontally, whereas in Vienna the vertical storey-addition is the equivalent favored method of enlarging the building fabric. Nevertheless, while the backyard extension at the rear of a terraced house constitutes a constructionally autonomous element, and as such can be evolved relatively simply, the roof extension, on the other hand, represents a far more challenging and delicate task, both in terms of urban planning and building regulations, as well as viewed from the perspective of its structural behavior. It is also remarkable that, compared to London, where backyard annexes most commonly take the form of a simply cubic volume, Vienna's rooftop extensions generate a particularly heterogeneous collection of architectural expressive forms. The question that therefore poses itself is why the rooftop landscape above the city to a greater extent excites a freer design idiom than the informal situation of the backyard.

---

1   See Steen Eiler Rasmussen, *London: The Unique City,* abridged version of the revised edition of 1937 (Harmondsworth: 1960), p. 15: "Two chief types are distinguishable among large cities: the concentrated and the scattered. The former is the more common on the continent and is clearly represented the big government seats of Paris and Vienna, which were the prototypes of European town planning at the end of the last century. The second type is represented by the English town [i. e. London], which now [1934] seems to many of us the ideal."

One possible explanation is the legacy of the Viennese avant-garde and its concentration on non-conformist spatial concepts. An early example that drew attention to Vienna's roof landscape was Hans Hollein's 1960 collage *Überbauung Wien* (*Superstructure above Vienna*). Its representation consists of a series of cloud forms, towering massively above the homogenous stone-built perimeter-block structure of the city as the emblem of a new and liberated urban form.[2] What follows below is a comparative discussion of three iconic rooftop extensions, which despite their differences in architectural approach and understanding can all be traced back to this basic idea of the Viennese avant-garde. What is also striking is the fact that steel—deployed in Vienna's rooftop extensions mostly in a profane manner as a pragmatic load-bearing framework in combination with wood—plays a key role in all three projects in terms of their spatial effect and in being highly articulated in terms of their construction.

PSYCHOGRAM IN STEEL AND GLASS

The early creative phase of Coop Himmelb(l)au,[3] with its focus on prototypical spatial structures for a future perspective "open society," exemplarily embodies the original spirit of the Viennese avant-garde of the 1960s and 1970s.[4] To begin with, the office pursued a vision of the autonomous object, consisting of pneumatic spheres,[5] but very shortly afterwards these ephemeral spatial ideas came to be anchored in direct association with pre-existing structures.[6] It could be argued that the architect group's core focus evolved towards an implementation within the urban environment, and by the same token away from the avant-garde's original individualistic vision of mobility. Be that as it may, whereas the pneumatic projects were innocent and soft interventions, the architectural duo of Prix and Swiczinsky began, as of the early 1980s, to evolve a considerably more aggressive architectural idiom with the aim of violently transforming the underlying fabric of the city. The manifesto for this new architectural approach made its appearance in 1980 in the form of their installation, or better said happening, *Flammenflügel* (*The Blazing Wing*). The piece involved the hanging of an approximately 15-meter-tall steel construction above the courtyard of the TU Graz, which was then set on fire via ignition gas valves: and despite the use of "water curtains" as a safety measure, the initiation of the work resulted in the de-

---

2   See Hans Hollein and Walter Pichler, *Hollein – Pichler – Architektur,* exhibition catalog for Galerie St. Stephan (Vienna: 1963). "The development of humanity is embodied in the city. Man, who stands on the highest rung of civilization and culture, strives for an even more concentrated, even more compacted city, an even more natural, even less developed land. Today we can finally leave our wretched huts and move to the cities, which float majestically and powerfully above the land or, compressed and concentrated, dig themselves at various points into the earth."

3   The architecture office was founded in 1968 by Wolf D. Prix, Michael Holzer and Helmut Swiczinsky (with Holzer remaining until 1971).

4   Wolf D. Prix, 20th Vienna Architecture Congress, Architekturzentrum Wien, Nov. 19, 2016.

5   For instance the projects Villa Rosa (1968) or Group-Dynamic Housing Organism (1969–1970).

6   For instance in the projects Fresh Cells for the City (1972–1973) and The House with the Flying Roof (1973).

TECHNOLOGICAL EUPHORIA   86

struction of most of the surrounding windows of the university building.[7] This introduction was followed by a number of realized remodeling projects on *Gründerzeit*-era buildings, such as the bar Roter Engel (1981) and the Studio Baumann (1985), in which steel constructions colonized existing spaces and repatterned them. This period culminated in 1988 in their key work, the rooftop extension on Falkestrasse.[8] At first glance it looks as if an over-dimensional alien object of steel and glass, lightly jutting out over the street, had landed on the roof of an inner-city *Gründerzeit*-era tenement building. Whereas the two previously mentioned remodeling projects operated at street level, and drilled through the base areas of each of their "host bodies," the rooftop extension allowed the architects to come noticeably closer to realizing the idea of a weightless architecture. Wolf D. Prix, who elucidated Coop Himmelb(l)au's methods in a lecture in London at the time, spoke in terms of built psychograms in which the primary design principle consisted of the shimmering line.[9] In this context he mentioned, making direct reference to Sigmund Freud: "As we, Coop Himmelblau, are Viennese, we have a close connection to Freud, who taught us that suppression requires a tremendous amount of energy. We would like to expend this energy on projects."[10] Based on intuition and emotional energy, spatial figures such as these were in turn organized and translated into a complex load-bearing framework by the structural engineer Oskar Graf—according to Prix, the real deconstructivist among the team.[11]

In concrete terms, the centerpiece of the rooftop extension is the meeting room of the legal firm, consisting of a two-story-high glazed room with a side gallery. The primary geometry of the project is defined by a diagonally spanned, curved main girder, which cantilevers slightly over the edge of the building to form an arch out into the street space and back to the stairwell. Seen in terms of construction, this element is in fact an articulated beam that is spanned backwards at both ends. In contrast, to the sides the partly glazed and partly closed roof areas are formed using simple girders, which are spanned between the mid-wall and specially shaped steel edge girders. These edge girders, which act as brackets, are connected to a floor slab made of reinforced concrete, which in turn counters the shearing forces. Transversely, the main girder is fixed, in comparison, using member bars. Alongside the aforementioned gallery, which also gives the entrance a spatial emphasis, a

7   "The distorted steel construction, 15 meters high and weighing 1.5 tons, was developed to be fueled by liquid gas burners. The wing was suspended in the courtyard of the Technical University in Graz on December 12, 1980, and was ignited at 8.35 pm. Water curtains protected the façades. During the action the crackling of the flames was heard over amplifiers." http://www.coophimmelblau.at/architecture/projects/theblazingwing/ (accessed March 16, 2017).

8   The original design was produced in 1983.

9   Wolf D. Prix (Coop Himmelblau), "On the Edge," in *AD Architectural Design Profile,* 87, no. 60/9–10 (1990): *Deconstruction III,* ed. Andreas C. Papadakis, pp. 65–70.

10   Ibid., p. 65.

11   Ibid., p. 67: "Although it is not immediately important, construction becomes crucial at the second or third step. In order to build this suspended, floating feeling, you have to know about more than columns and beams. In fact, our structural engineer is the only real deconstructionist in our group; only he knows how to calculate by separating every part and then can put it back together again."

6

7

8

9

10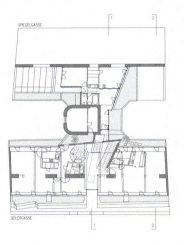

Rüdiger Lainer + Partner, penthouse, Seilergasse 16, 1995.
A striking steel structure with T-shaped girders positioned
obliquely to the façade and balanced on the central wall
of the existing building.
Structural-framework planning: Helmuth Locher

TECHNOLOGICAL EUPHORIA 88

so-called saw-tooth shed roof—a zigzag-shaped sheet-steel element—and a terrace at the corner of the building form the subsidiary areas, which give the building an extra pattern. Seen as a whole, the main room looks—in keeping with the general objective given by Prix—polydimensional and uninhibitedly impulsive. Simultaneously, an element of deliberate irony appears inevitable in this connection: a conference room has been created that displays a highly destabilizing spatial situation, but which at second glance proves, in construction terms, to form an enormously complex and refined interweaving of lines of force. The result is that it would appear as if the architecture is depicting the legal hurdles facing the client and the corresponding stress situation in the form of an ambiguous spatial representation.

BALANCING STRUCTURAL FRAMEWORK AND FLUCTUATING SPACES

Starting in the early 1990s, and thanks to the political tide change in Eastern Europe and the fall of the Iron Curtain, Vienna experienced an intensified building boom, accompanied architecturally—probably also as a counter-reaction to the deconstructivism of the 1980s—by a shift towards a certain pragmatism. Echoing the international zeitgeist, the predominant language of form in Vienna became a neo-modernist linearity, but one that expressed itself as a characteristic local phenomenon in its refusal to completely abandon its claims to an avant-garde radicalism. The office founded by Rüdiger Lainer in the mid-1980s was one of just this category of architects who deployed an ambiguous vocabulary, mixing minimalism with deconstructivism.[12] As one of their first building commissions, in 1995 Lainer realized a large roof-top extension located on the Seilergasse in Vienna's city center. The project encompasses a double-story heightening of a building from the *Gründerzeit* era only a few strides away from the Stephansdom. Despite the fundamental differences in terms of its overall expression, it can in fact be compared to the design topics of the lawyer's office in Falkestrasse in relation to the formal contrast to the existing building, the dissolution of space, and a destabilizing interior spatial hierarchy.

The architects' main aim was to erect a neutral spatial structure with a façade as open and column-free as possible.[13] This goal was realized by applying an ingenious construction principle that saw the use of balancing steel T-girders running transversely to the main alignment of the building. These girders rest on an existing mid-wall, enabling trapezoidal sheet metal with concrete topping to be spanned longitudinally as floor slabs between them.[14] This simple yet at the same time succinct construction method can be read in relation to the conventional building techniques used in the existing building, involving timber load-bearing floors, each of them spanned between the masonry of the outer and central walls. To this extent, the new

12 Office in Vienna as of 1985.
13 See Ingerid Helsing Almaas, *Vienna: Objects and Rituals* (Cologne: 1997), p. 10.
14 Additional cylindrical columns are selectively positioned as stabilization on the ground floor and towards the courtyard in the upper story.

11

13

12

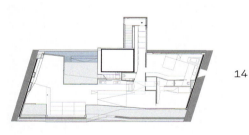

14

Delugan Meissl Associated Architects, Ray 1, Mittersteig, 2003.
The themes of floating and folding are realized by means
of a complex steel structure. A steel grid divides the load of the
extension between as many points as possible in the existing
1960s building below.
Structural-framework planning: Werkraum ZT GmbH

TECHNOLOGICAL EUPHORIA

primary construction can be interpreted as a radical refinement of the building principles of the *Gründerzeit,* albeit in this case by applying a constructional-steelwork method. As a conclusion to the building, it is topped by a separate space-containing façade element with a narrow glazed roof, forming the transitional point between the loft-like inner space and the surrounding roofscape of Vienna's city center.

This spatial membrane, however, which considered in isolation is both neutral and generous, has a number of architectural interventions contrapuntally superimposed over it, resulting in the creation of a complex spatial object. The most obvious examples are the differently slanting partition walls and annexes, the latter forming the subsidiary rooms facing the courtyard, such as the bedrooms, kitchen, bathrooms, and meeting rooms.[15] The soberness of the spatial membrane is likewise contradicted by the sculptural interior fliers, constructed in concrete, aluminum, and wood, with point-fixed glass railings. Last but not least, the previously noted minimized structural-glazing façade is equipped with conspicuous natural-wood frames that serve as opening casements. On the one hand, and seen from outside, these terrace doors lend the otherwise minimalist face a graphic articulation, and also indirectly constitute a formal connection to the window formats of the historic building below. On the other hand, as a correction, or rather a countermeasure, they likewise invest the open surface and what would otherwise be the exteriorly exposed interior rooms a certain spatial stability.[16] The interplay between these subsidiary interventions and the elementary appearance of the prime structure creates a spatial tension and a contradiction, which can be interpreted as deliberate irritations: as if the rooftop extension were trying to consciously emphasize an architectural embodiment of the schizophrenic relationship between residential living and work, old and new, intimate rooms and the fully glazed amenity spaces, and, finally, the confusion between inner protectiveness and a theatrical extroversion.[17]

FLOATING FOLDED SLAB

The last of the three iconic rooftop extensions is the project Ray 1 by Elke Delugan Meissl and Roman Delugan, designed as their own family apartment and completed in 2003. Whereas the two previously discussed rooftop extensions are enlargements to typical late-*Gründerzeit* apartment buildings, the existing building in this case is a 1960s six-story office building with a

---

15 One motive for this deconstructivist speciality could be a formal play of the sightlines and the reference axes. This principal of an "open system" reappears in Rüdiger Lainer's lead urban-planning object Altes Flugfeld Aspern. See https://www.lainer.at/wp/wpcontent/ uploads/037aspern2.pdf (accessed March 16, 2017).

16 Almaas, *Vienna* (see note 13), p. 10.

17 Ibid., p. 11: "Nothing here mediates between water taps of the door handle and the city. […] Lying, for instance, naked in the whirlpool in the rear room, you can open a hatch window and look out over the Stephansdom; push this highly discreet pane of glass to one side, and this Middle Age stone giant assumes an entirely new significance: it is not simply a House of God, a tourist attraction, but rather it joins in with the warm bath, as lifelike as the bubbling, splashing water and the smell of the soap. Here in your bath, with a view of the Stephansdom, you are quite simply unbeatable. That's how fantastic a city can be."

reinforced-concrete skeleton construction and ribbon-window façades. Although, as distinct from the other two projects, the contrast between the old building and the new is less pronounced in terms of the manner of construction, nevertheless this rooftop extension can similarly be read as an oppositional figure. It could be argued that the design by Delugan Meissl is an eccentric advancement of the architectural principle of the host building, in which the formal correlation between the old and the new constitutes the core theme. The motifs that are reused in the rooftop extension are, first and foremost, the ribbon windows and the stressing of the horizontality of the space. However, in contrast to the functional rationality of the window arrangement and spatial structure of the office stories, these topics are then heightened in the penthouse in order to allow a stretched spatial impact to evolve.

The wave-like silhouette of the rooftop extension is generated by joining the two differently tall gable ends of the adjoining fire walls. Simultaneously, this buckled line has the effect of visualizing the primary direction of span of the load-bearing roof construction—a geometrically complex steel structure made of kneed single and trussed girders. At various junctures, for instance in the bedroom area, additional steel supports have been inserted, concealed within the walls, in turn supported on a volumetric steel girder grille. By virtue of its varying height profile, this load-spreading floor slab acts as the spatial counterpart to the form of the roof. Between these two elements, a fluid, free-span space unfolds, in which the floor traces the ascending spiral progression from the entrance upward via the kitchen to the living and dining areas with the roof terrace. A further important motif realized in the project is the principle of hovering. This is primarily apparent in the living area between the kitchen and the dining area, where the surface of the roof folds itself in a faceted arching movement towards the wall section and downward to the horizontal level below, before finally then floating above the actual floor. The approximately 15-centimeter-high seam between the plateau and the floor is formed by a strip window at the height of the base, which also acts as a load-bearing element. Seen from the exterior, the element has the appearance of a dormer. It is carried by the parapet of the terrace extending in front of it, which in turn is a trussed girder covered in sheet steel, and which, in sync with the hovering principle, spans the entire 14 meters of the building's length.

This third example of an iconic rooftop extension can be positioned in relationship to a central aspect of Josef Frank's reasoning. Frank, one of most relevant Viennese early-modern architects, declared in his 1931 essay "Das Haus als Weg und Platz" (The House as Path and Place) that the ideal of the modern apartment house could be traced back to the bohemian attic studio. In these unplanned residuals of the apartment block are to be found the spatial qualities that modernism was searching for: "Large rooms, large windows, many corners, crooked walls, steps and differences in levels, columns, beams—in short all the diversity that we are looking for in the New

House in order to escape the dreary barrenness of the rectangular room."[18] This description is, at first sight, also applicable to Ray 1. Nevertheless, the marked difference between Frank's notion of an informal architecture and that of Delugan Meissl lies in the question of secureness and sentimentality. Already in 1927, as a critique of the austere architecture of the Weissen-hofsiedlung, Frank had written: "One can't always live at the climaxes of things; each person his own particular measure of sentimentality that he has to satisfy."[19] While the common mansard, due to its relaxed atmosphere, permits this, in contradiction to Frank's statement the rooftop extension on Mittersteig generates a transcending spatial principle that can be interpreted as a consciously unsentimental architectural idea.

INNER LANDSCAPES OVER THE METROPOLIS

What makes each of the rooftop extensions described above unusual and yet comparable is the connection between their effusive spatial and occupancy concepts and the steel constructions that spatially enable the designs to be undertaken in the first place. A second common aspect is their particularly intensive relation to the urban fabric. The three roof extensions all pursue the spatial idea of capturing the wideness of the roofscape within their built spatial structures. However, this eccentric architecture also illustrates a problematic aspect that as a critique applies to the Viennese rooftop extension in general, namely that these are projects that cultivate an architectural accentuation in order to rise above their surroundings—in other words a private architecture that exhibits a parasitical relationship to the overall shape of the city. To summarize, what these architects have managed to achieve with their rooftop extensions is to erect buildings that embody the idea of floating above the city, and in that sense have accomplished the architectural realization of Hans Hollein's collage *Superstructure over Vienna* in the form of a private utopia. And, due to its property of being a shapable line of force, steel as a building material constitutes the crucial basis for the accentuated spatial concepts of these late-avant-garde rooftop extensions.

18   Josef Frank, "Das Haus als Weg und Platz," in *Der Baumeister,* 8 (1931), pp. 316–323, as cited in Tano Bojankin, Christopher Long, and Iris Meder (eds.), *Josef Frank: Schriften in zwei Bänden* (Vienna: 2012), vol. 2, p. 198.
19   Josef Frank, "Der Gschnas fürs G'müt und der Gschnas als Problem," in Deutscher Werkbund (ed.), *Bau und Wohnung Ausstellungskatalog* (Stuttgart: 1927), pp. 48–57, as cited in Bojankin, Long, and Meder, *Josef Frank* (see note 18), vol. 1, p. 288.

TECHNOLOGICAL EUPHORIA

Taming the Future in the Tube

The Design for the Extension of the Kunstakademie Düsseldorf by Karl Wimmenauer, Lyubo-Mir Szabo, and Ernst Kasper in 1968
Martin Tschanz

In fall 1968, practically simultaneously, the journals *Architecture d'Aujourd'hui* and *Werk* both published details of an extension project for the Kunstakademie Düsseldorf. The gigantic double tube made of transparent plastic, which would appear to float above the old historic building, caused a sensation. Soon afterwards, *L'architettura—cronache e storia* likewise showed this "*soluzione shockante,*" and with its inclusion by Heinrich Klotz in his canonical 1986 exhibition *Vision der Moderne—Das Prinzip Konstruktion* (Visions of Modernism—The Principle of Construction) it advanced to find its final place in the architecture history of the twentieth century.[1]

Even today, the project continues to exercise a fascination, perhaps precisely because despite its imaginal force it remains impossible to grasp at a single glance. Is it a design drawn up to provide a real solution to the academy's notoriously cramped conditions, but ultimately never realized for simple "legal reasons"[2]—as suggested in the journals? Or is it not instead a utopian project? Does it address the issue of the vertical city? Or is it better understood as an academic finger exercise in how to treat existing architectural substance?

THE CONTEXT OF THE KUNSTAKADEMIE DÜSSELDORF

In 1968, the lack of space in the academy was indisputable and acute. The old building by Hermann Riffart and Wilhelm Lotz, erected between 1875 and 1879 and which in many respects borrowed from Semper's building for the Polytechnical School in Zurich, had long been bursting at the seams. As early as 1929, Emil Fahrenkamp had not only planned an annex building but likewise a vertical extension.[3] In the course of the general reconstruction following World War II, the roof space did indeed undergo an expansion, whereby it noticeably failed to relieve the permanent severe overcrowding, as did the insertion of gallery levels into the studio spaces.

Thereby there was no lack of ideas of how to obtain additional space. In its issue for winter 1966/67, the academy newspaper *Nachrichten Bilder Berichte* collected a variety of complementary proposals, which "our architects" had elaborated over the previous years, in part together with their students.[4] Despite having occupied the academy's professorial chair for New Architectural History and Design since 1963, Karl Wimmenauer was not a participant in this process.[5]

TECHNOLOGICAL EUPHORIA

THE EXTENSION BY KARL WIMMENAUER, LYUBO-MIR SZABO, AND ERNST KASPER

The project that Wimmenauer developed in 1968, together with Lyubo-Mir Szabo and his office partner Ernst Kasper,[6] may in this sense have served as a vehicle with which to intervene in the on-going discussion and to stake his claim vis-à-vis their rivals in order to attract a commission. Simultaneously, however, it also represented a public critique of the projects that had already been formulated by his colleagues. Along with extensions on adjoining plots, these projects had proposed various different adjuncts to the old academy, designed either to accommodate ateliers and lecture theaters on the western side projections[7] or for additional ancillary rooms on the north side of the building. Entailing a new spatial stratum, these projects would have resulted in transforming the single-flush complex into a double-flush one.[8]

Wimmenauer's team rejected these approaches,[9] basing their reasons for doing so on fundamental considerations. The historic building, the explanatory project report pointed out, was "worthy of preservation in conservation terms," and further: "Quite apart from the rich tradition of its artistic past, the college is eminently usable as a generously laid-out studio building, meaning that there is no reason to emasculate and dismember its substance, or for that matter to completely abandon it, with yet more insertions and annexes."[10]

Instead, therefore, the proposal was "to provide an extension of the academy *above* the existing building [...] but at no point whatsoever to interfere with the substance of the preservation-worthy monument." There could be "no possible idea" of "equating this with a heightening of the building in the conventional sense of an alteration of the contours." On the contrary, the design considered the "historic academy, as both an artistic institution and a monument deserving conservation, [...] to be the substructure of the new architectural thought."[11] The project could therefore, the report argued, serve as a model and nucleus for the handling of the historic fabric of the city in the future.

Numerous sketches in Wimmenauer's bequest prove that this idea of an autonomous new object above the old one constituted the core of the design. A few of the drawings show the new as a megastructure that adopts individual characteristics of the arrangement of the existing in a type of mirroring effect. The majority of them, however, demonstrate the search for an autonomous and highly concise configuration. They depict, for example, a type of city over the city with its own individual silhouette, or varieties of ship, or a futuristic fantasy form (figs. 1-4).

It is probably no coincidence that these drawings echo Hans Hollein's early collages in which he placed such forms as petrified clouds or eroded bones above the city, or made them swim as aircraft carriers in a bucolic landscape (see title image to the chapter "The Psychology of the High-Flyer," pp. 82-83).[12] Hollein had arrived at the Kunstakademie Düsseldorf a year earlier as the successor to Hans Schwippert, and Wimmenauer may well have therefore been acquainted with his work, including his *Vision of a City* and *Communication Interchange* (1962/63) in which Hollein had deployed the motif of a double-tube feeding out high in the air.

ARCHITECTURE PARLANTE

The design by Wimmenauer, Szabo, and Kasper is distinctly memorable and evocative. This corresponds to its presentation. There are no conventional plans; instead these are substituted by the use of the various potentials of suggestive, artistic medias. The spectrum stretches from a scheme of the outline of the city seen from a bird's-eye perspective, sketched over in heavy pencil, to elaborate photomontages, realized in the academy's photo-studio by Mladen Lipecky, to an etching that Wimmenauer has signed as if it were an art print. The latter condenses the entire project in all its variations together, represented in elevation and cross-section sketches, perspectives and diagrams (fig. 7). In addition, the Karl Wimmenauer Bequest in the Deutsche Architekturmuseum in Frankfurt includes an expressive ball-point-pen drawing, in which the handwriting and the hatching seamlessly intermesh, as well as a no-less-expressive large-format perspective collage by the artist and academy professor Rupprecht Geiger, in which the end faces of the superstructure become bright-orange, circular fields of color.

These images imminently suggest that the project should be interpreted symbolically: the twin-tube as a giant pair of binoculars and the academy, as an institution, looking sharply into the far future assisted by this instrument. This reading would be implicit in some of the presentations in the way in which the tubes are accentuated through their articulated ends or their apparent rotatability. Simultaneously, it forcibly occurs to the viewer to see the project as a fragment of a tunnel system, as a type of subway system suspended in the air. This could be read as an expression of the new status of art and the artist in society, a topic that was under intense discussion at the time in the academy. In that case, the project would be an utterance of the fact that the sphere of art no longer belonged in the Palace of Art, but nor that it belonged underground: instead it belonged in the overground, visible for miles around, networking the city. Similarly, the hierarchical placing of new and old side by side, or rather stacked on top of each other, coupled with the demonstrative conservation of the old academy, could be correspondingly understood as programmatic. The new extends the old

and ascends above it, but by no means substitutes it: instead it exploits it and requires it as a base and a foundation. In the case of Karl Wimmenauer, for whom Claude-Nicolas Ledoux was an important reference,[13] such an interpretation of the project as *architecture parlante* would certainly seem reasonable.

On an axonometric urban view of Düsseldorf[14] the architects superimpose a drawn network of tubes, starting from the academy, that connects the blocks of the city center over their rooftops (fig. 5). Accordingly, the seventh and final point of their "project rationale" reads: "The new architectural idea can reproduce itself, radiating from its point of origin. Existing urban neighborhoods and streets are no longer 'modernized' bit by bit, instead serving, with their historic substance, as a substructure for a elevated pedestrian city, which multiplies urban capacity."

With this aspect the project also joins the discussion about the three-dimensional city, which at the time was in full swing. However, as opposed to the urban visions of Constant, Yona Friedman, and others, who proposed open and dynamic structures, the Düsseldorf project instead envisions a closed, basically hermetic system. The new was to be connected to the old only selectively and via sluice-like-shaped threshold spaces. It was only on the inside that the dynamics of future activities could run wild, accommodated by replenishing the basic structure according to the corresponding momentary, specific requirements. Nevertheless, everything remains enclosed within the plastic tubes, as if the existing world had to be optimally shielded from the coming one. By transferring it to the normality of the city as a whole, the problematic nature of the philosophy of building preservation at the time becomes fully apparent, namely the tendency to isolate a monument in favor of a clear legibility and to freeze it in the name of maximal retention of substance.

While appearing compact and hermetic from the outside, the tubes' inner workings were conceived as free and anarchic: "The installation—using a lightweight construction—of one-man cells to large class-studios is to be undertaken by the users themselves according to their needs, and are intended to be easily modifiable."[15] This has echoes of Lyubo-Mir Szabo's programmatic concept in a 1967 ideas competition for the University of Bremen,[16] in which he and his team designed not a building but instead, obviously inspired by Cedric Price, a "novel, mechanical-like topological conglomerate of building and learning processes"[17]—a framework with powerful crane runways that allowed containers to be arranged in a state of permanent transformation.

The spatial concept for the Kunstakademie Düsseldorf was not quite so radical, but the model of the project likewise shows a skeleton in which platforms, ceilings, or room cells could be implemented either as required or ad lib. The likes of Beuys or Hollein could run riot in the tubes, simultaneously exposed and locked up like ants in a terrarium.

UTOPIA OR REALIZABLE PROJECT?

The manifesto-like, utopian character of the design is counterpoised by two expert technical reports that give the appearance of demonstrating the feasibility of the project. The in-depth domestic engineering report by INTEGRAL Architekten und Ingenieure GmbH[18] was basically positive: "In terms of installations [...] there are no particular concerns [...] about the proposed architectural conceptualization." In detail, however, the verdict was damning. Laconically, it was noted that a "cladding [...] with transparent material (Zellodur?)" was "not feasible in terms of energy efficiency."[19] "Today's industry would already be able," claimed the architects in their explanatory report, to supply "high-quality elastic materials" that "automatically become clouded in the sunlight and that guarantee complete heat and sound insulation"[20]—an optimism that the engineers evidently did not share.

As far as the load-bearing structure was concerned, engineer Stefan Polónyi confirmed that a dispersion of the forces via transverse steel frames onto the numerous intermediate walls of the old building was feasible, and that the existing foundations were capable of bearing the additional loads. His proposal for the tube-shaped skin took the form of a structural frame of longitudinal girders with transverse tendons at 2.2-meter intervals that would have required being joined with the primary frame at points. "Double-shell acrylic-glass or Celludor circular-ring-sectional shell elements" were to act as an "intermediate layer."[21]

There is a clear discrepancy between the tubular structure of the design and its load-bearing structure. The separation of the tube-shaped skin from the transverse, almost crosswall-like primary structure would have never have been sufficient for the twin tubes to be spanned in a bridge form from building block to building block, or to position them diagonally above the academy as the project suggested.

There is various evidence that the architects indeed drew up their project in response to what was the real and concrete problem of the academy's urgent need for space, but that they never seriously worked towards their design being realizable. The only drawing in Karl Wimmenauer's papers that shows a double-shell skin in the sense that Polónyi suggested is marked "Version 1" and was never published (fig. 6). What this drawing underlines is how extremely a constructional detailing of the project would have detracted from its original character. Contrary to this, the 1:200-scale model, which constituted the core of the project and was used as a basis for the technical expertise,[22] remained schematic in relation to both the skin and the structural framework, and was instead cosmetically beautified to emphasize a transparent, floating effect (`fig. 8` and `fig. 9`: photomontage, models and photos of the old building). Even a coordination of framework axes between the old and the new building was dispensed with, and the ultra-thin mini-supports between the two constructions—needless to say minus cross-bracing—made no effort whatsoever to emulate a credible structural framework. By the same token, however, this in turn reinforced the demonstrative disconnected sovereignties of the old and the new that was so crucial to the project's authors.[23]

Moreover, apparently the architects initially decided against submitting their project to the academy. A letter by Wimmenauer implies that director Eduard Trier first became aware of the project when it was published. Wimmenauer wrote that he was compiling a folder with the "material" that had been "sent to a number of journals for publication,"[24] emphasizing that it had been pointed out to the respective editors "that the project was no longer tenable for building-regulation reasons" and that the design had been created "independently of a building commission."[25]

This last point would certainly explain why, as opposed to the official extension projects, Wimmenauer's design was left unmentioned in the 1973 commemorative publication *Zweihundert Jahre Kunstakademie Düsseldorf.*[26] It was only in 2013 that it became part of the school's official record, published in *Die Geschichte der Kunstakademie Düsseldorf seit 1945* with reference to the above-mentioned presentation by Heinrich Klotz in 1986.[27] Without the retrospective efforts of the Deutsche Architekturmuseum during the flowering of postmodernism to preserve such testimonies, it would have no doubt shared the same fate as most of the other utopian projects of its era and would have sunk into oblivion.

The design for the extension of the Kunstakademie Düsseldorf demonstrates the power that a project can accrue by liberating itself from complexity and the compulsions of reality. To this extent, the attempts by the engineer to resolve its program in a physical load-bearing structure, which continues what exists, has an undoubtedly invigorating effect in terms of its pragmatism, but nonetheless inevitably contradicts the essential nature of the project. This lies in the abrupt antithesis between old and new, coupled with a simultaneous vagueness of the new.

Inherently, each architectural addition to an existing substance compels the architect to assume a stance on history. At particular times it was customary to ideally bring the old to disappear; in others the aspiration was to amalgamate within the traditional, or it was considered self-evident that the old and the new should exist in combination, the new extending or substituting the old by using the respective current methods. In the project in Düsseldorf, on the other hand, old and new are mutually divorced and placed next to, or rather on top of one another. This moment of detachment occurs not only spatially but in certain respects also temporally, in the sense that the new is shifted from the here and now towards the future.

Not only despite, but also precisely because of its futuristic demeanor, the project proves itself to be a precursor of postmodernist sensitivities. Here, the past and the future occur simultaneously and in the present day, devoid of any prospect of succession. Just like an antique guarantees a modern milieu its newness,[28] so this futuristic object banishes the future and reinforces the old in its perpetual validity.

1 "Aktuell" column, in *Werk,* 55, no. 11 (1968), n. p.; "aa actualités," in *L'Architecture d'Aujourd'hui,* 140 (Oct./Nov. 1968), p. LXIV; *L'architettura—cronache e storia,* XIV, no. 162/12 (April 1969), pp. 878–879; Heinrich Klotz, *Vision der Moderne: Das Prinzip Konstruktion* (Munich: 1986), pp. 256–263.

2 *L'Architecture d'Aujourd'hui* and *L'architettura* (see note 1).

3 Christoph Heuter, *Emil Fahrenkamp 1885–1966: Architekt im rheinisch-westfälischen Industriegebiet* (Petersberg: 2002), p. 298.

4 Walter Köngeter, "Raumnot," in *Hochschule für Bildende Künste—Nachrichten Bilder Berichte,* 2 (Winter Semester 1966/67). The annual publication is a simple leaflet.

5 Kunstakademie Düsseldorf (ed.), *Die Geschichte der Kunstakademie Düsseldorf seit 1945* (Munich: 2013).

6 Collaborator: Wolfgang Meyer; structural engineering: Stefan Polónyi; technical consultation: INTEGRAL Architekten und Ingenieure.

7 Auditorium and workshops on the north side: student projects supervised by Prof. Schwippert and Prof. Köngeter, 1964–1966; studio and workshop building on the south side: student projects supervised by Prof. Schwarz / Faber, 1955. See Köngeter, "Raumnot" (see note 4). The studio building designed by Rudolf Schwarz and built in 1956 to 1958, also known as the "Steinhaus," was originally intended to have been connected with the main building. See Agatha Buslei-Wuppermann, "Geschichte und räumliche Erweiterungen seit 1945," in Kunstakademie Düsseldorf (ed.), *Geschichte der Kunstakademie Düsseldorf* (see note 5), pp. 398–408, here p. 404.

8 Prof. Schwippert / Staatshochbauamt, 1961. See Köngeter, "Raumnot" (see note 4).

9 Sketches in the Karl Wimmenauer Bequest in the Deutsches Architekturmuseum (DAM) Frankfurt verify that the possibility of annex buildings had been actively entertained.

10 "Erläuterungsbericht," signed Wimmenauer, Szabo, and Kasper, Düsseldorf, June 2, 1968, p. 2: Wimmenauer Bequest, DAM, and Akademie Düsseldorf, Archive.

11 Ibid., p. 3.

12 For instance *Superstructure above Vienna* (1960), *Superstructure above Manhattan* (1963) or *Aircraft-Carrier-City in the Landscape* (1964). These titles and dates are taken from the website www.hollein.com (accessed Feb. 22, 2017), but vary from publication to publication.

13 Buslei-Wuppermann describes Ledoux as Wimmenauer's favorite architect. See Buslei-Wuppermann, "Geschichte und räumliche Erweiterungen" (see note 7). In Wimmenaur's writings, the mentions of Ledoux do in fact increase with time.

14 "Düsseldorf—Drawn from May to October 1957 by Hermann Bollmann—Revised in 1962": Wimmenauer Bequest, DAM.

15 "Erläuterungsbericht" (see note 10), p. 3.

16 *Architektur Wettbewerbe,* special issue no. 5 (1968): *Universität Bremen,* pp. 94–96; *Bauwelt,* 42/43 (1967), pp. 1053–1075, esp. pp. 1056, 1067. The design was drawn by Lyubo-Mir Szabo, Wolfgang Rathke, and Heinz Behrendt.

17 [Lyubo-Mir] Szabo, für die Anonyme Arbeitsgemeinschaft Testament, Mutterzelle Wuppertal, "Planart," in Rolf Wedewer and Thomas Kempas, *Architektonische Spekulationen* (Düsseldorf: 1970), n. p. The publication

18 also mentions the extension project for the academy, illustrating it with two accompanying model photos. For the design for Bremen, see also Sonja Hnilica, "Systeme und Strukturen: Universitätsbau in der BRD und das Vertrauen in die Technik," in *Wolkenkuckucksheim,* 19, no. 33 (2014), pp. 211–233, esp. p. 222: cloudcuckoo.net/fileadmin/ issues_en/issue_33/ article_hnilica.pdf (accessed Feb. 19, 2017).

18 On September 9, 1967, Wimmenauer gave an extensive lecture in the planning center of INTEGRAL Architekten und Ingenieure GmbH in Mettmann close to Düsseldorf on the topic "Architekt und Ingenieur": Akademie Düsseldorf, Archive, QZ Wimme 5. The expert's report may have been some sort of reciprocal gesture.

19 "INTEGRAL: Projekt Erweiterung der Staatl. Kunstakademie Düsseldorf – Energietechnische Vorschläge" (expert's report), p. 2: Wimmenauer Bequest, DAM, and Akademie Düsseldorf, Archive. It has proven impossible to definitively identify the material or materials referred to as "Zellodur" (in the INTEGRAL expert's report and/or "Celludor" (in Polónyi's expert's report). Work in plastics was in fashion: in summer semester 1968 an Institute for Plastics Treatment had been set up at the academy.

20 "Erläuterungsbericht" (see note 10), p. 3.

21 Stefan Polónyi, "Gutachten, Betr.: Aufstockung der Kunstakademie Düsseldorf," p. 2: Wimmenauer Bequest, DAM, and Akademie Düsseldorf, Archive.

22 The basis for their report was revealed by INTEGRAL to have been spoken discussions by the architects based on a 1:200 model. See INTEGRAL expert's report (see note 19), p. 2.

23 It would appear that in the model the architects had conjectured a different structural system, involving the service story as a type of widely spanned bridge between the projections of the old building, upon which the load-bearing frame was to rest, independently of the ballast structure of the old academy. In contrast, the rough section drawings, which were the only plan-like sketches to be published, illustrate the structural system described by Polónyi. The axonometry drawn especially for this publication combines aspects from the differing, divergent sources.

24 Karl Wimmenauer to Prof. Dr. Eduard Trier ("im Hause"), October 3, 1968: Kunstakademie Düsseldorf, Archive.

25 Ibid. Wimmenauer wrote "that the project is no longer tenable for building-regulation reasons, in particular also due to the fact the opportunities for extension within the immediate vicinity of the existing building would emerge that have only become known since the completion of the design." This argument would not appear to be all too convincing, especially because there cannot have been news of any possible extensions within the vicinity that would not have already been discussed in 1967.

26 Eva Brües, "Das Akademiegebäude," in Eduard Trier and Paul Böhringer (eds.), *Zweihundert Jahre Kunstakademie Düsseldorf* (Düsseldorf: 1973), pp. 127–138, here esp. p. 134.

27 Buslei-Wuppermann, "Geschichte und räumliche Erweiterungen seit 1945" (see note 7).

28 Cf. Jean Baudrillard, *The System of Objects,* trans. James Benedict (original French title: *Le système des objets,* 1968) (London and New York: 1996), esp. chap. B II: "A Marginal System: Collecting," pp. 85–106.

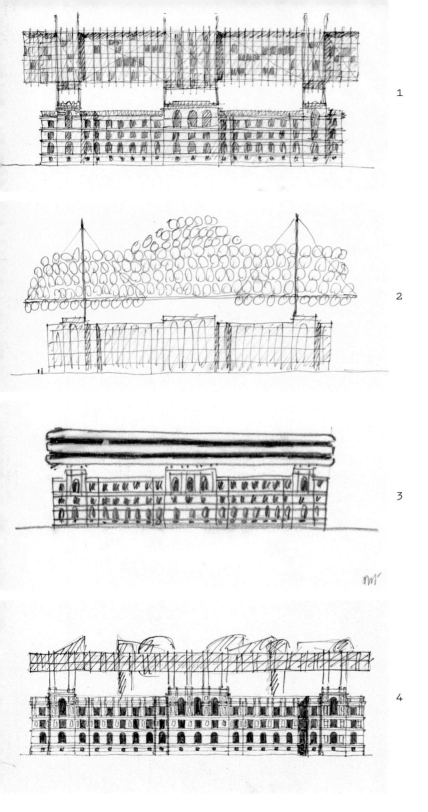

TECHNOLOGICAL EUPHORIA

1-4 Preliminary studies for a vertical extension of the Kunstakademie Düsseldorf in pencil and felt-tip pen by Karl Wimmenauer, 1968.
5 The concept of the tube as the starting point for the development of an elevated pedestrian city. Sketch overlaid on an axonometric overview of the city from the Karl Wimmenauer Bequest.

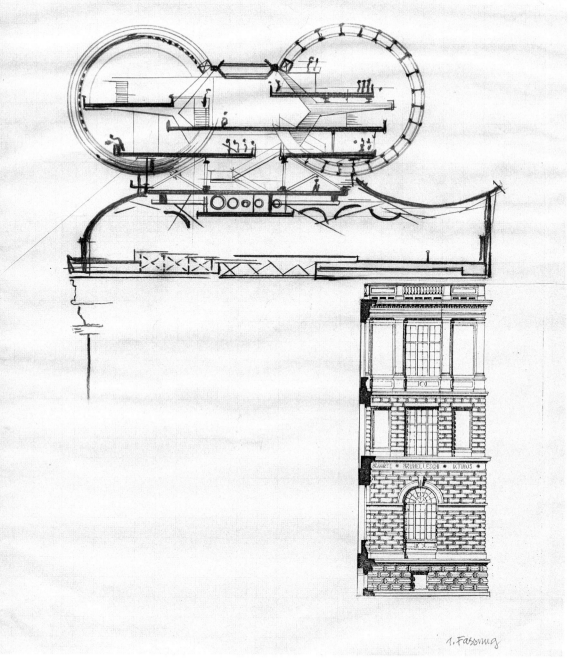

6 Utopia or realizable project? Technical sketch of the vertical extension of the Kunstakademie Düsseldorf from the Karl Wimmenauer Bequest.
7 Project sketch by Karl Wimmenauer in the form of an etching, 1968.

TECHNOLOGICAL EUPHORIA 104

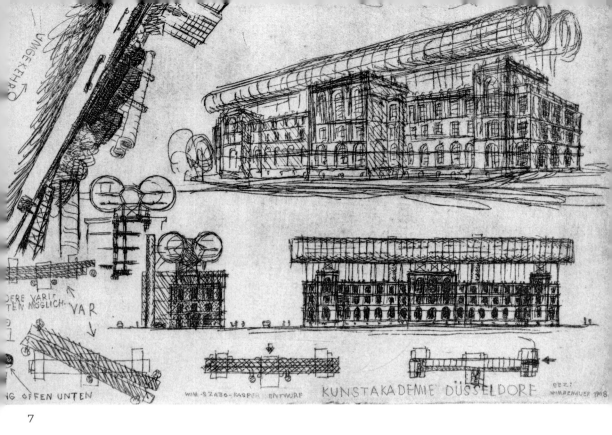

7

Photomontage using an architectural model, produced by the photographic studio at the academy by Mladen Lipecky, Düsseldorf, 1968.

TECHNOLOGICAL EUPHORIA

ENGINEERING COMMENTARY
DANIEL MEYER AND
PATRIC FISCHLI-BOSON

The central idea in the structural framework is the concept of transferring the additional loads via a row of supports on each crosswall in the substructure. The principle of this load distribution allows the bearing pressure to be raised evenly by almost a third. The consolidated floor would have tolerated this stress increase minus any additional reinforcement measures at foundation level. The structural framework was conceived as a steel frame, arranged on the supports at intervals of 6.6 meters diagonally to the building. In between were to be spans of prefabricated steel panels, bolted to the steel frame. Longitudinally, the bracing of the structural frame was secured by means of existing and newly designed elevator shafts and stairwells; diagonally by means of the frame action. The structural frame of the encasement was embedded in the 6.6-meter grid. Circular-shaped girders were to be arranged every 2.2 meters and mounted on either the frames or in between them via the respective longitudinal girders. An additional fixing of the frame was achieved using tension rods at the face end of the uppermost reinforced-concrete slab. It was intended to insert double-shell acrylic-glass or Celludor circular-ring-sectional shell elements between the load-bearing steel rings.

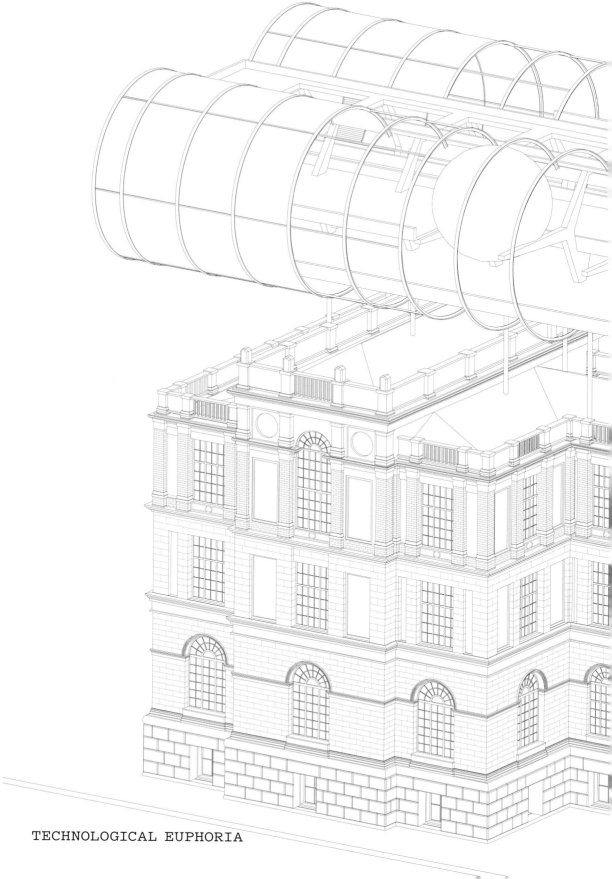

TECHNOLOGICAL EUPHORIA

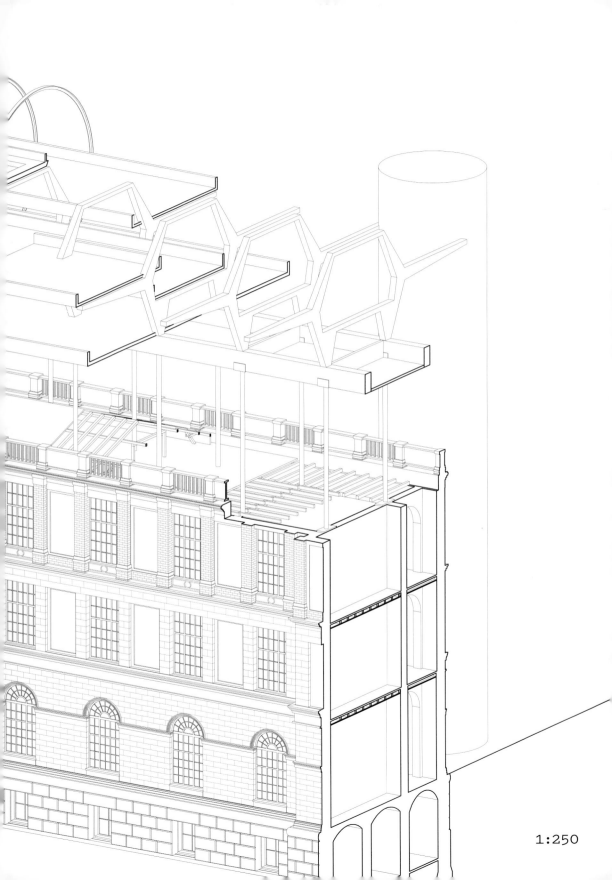

1:250

REDISCOVERY OF METAMORPHOSIS

Forme forte and the Picturesque Manner of Vertical Extension at the Turn of the Millennium

Patric Furrer   p. 112

History of Mining, Mining of History: The Design for the Reconstruction of the Zollverein Coal Mine, Shaft XII

Jürg Conzett and Roger Diener   p. 122

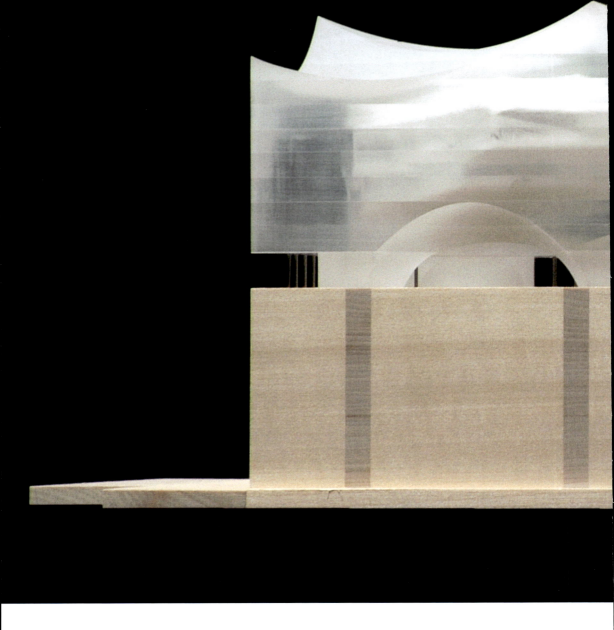

REDISCOVERY OF METAMORPHOSIS 112

1

2

Works such as *The Cube* by Alberto Giacometti (above),
or *Untitled (Cold Rolled Steel Boxes)* by Donald Judd (below)
as references for the concept of *forme forte*.

REDISCOVERY OF METAMORPHOSIS   114

Forme forte and the Picturesque Manner of Vertical Extension at the Turn of the Millennium

Patric Furrer

At the close of the twentieth century, a new tendency was established within building culture in Switzerland. *Forme forte* [powerful form] showed a way out of the postmodern crisis to an architecture no longer based on symbolic character, but rather on perceptual phenomena. Martin Steinmann bestowed it with a theoretical face, observing as a witness of the era: "In the architecture of the present, one may discern a tendency to form buildings of simple, clear volumes, as volumes that receive great meaning through simplicity of form, material, and color, and in fact without any reference to other buildings."[1] Architectural history itself no longer served as the reference point for this architecture. The principles and meanings of contemporary art acted as much more of an inspiration. Minimal art in particular became a source of inspiration for many architects. Notably, this engagement with the work of artists like Donald Judd or Alberto Giacometti directly manifested itself in the built work of Herzog & de Meuron. *The Cube* by Giacometti (fig. 1), or *Untitled* (*Six Cold Rolled Steel Boxes*) by Judd (fig. 2) are emblematic for the geometric simplicity of the type of objects that suppress any kind of tectonic through their surfaces. Thus a complex effect is produced through the surface effect, through the material aesthetic. With this new focus, the concept of the façade also changes. It is intensified as a "medium," understood as an image freed from supporting structure.[2]

At first glance, new construction and its capacity for unified expression comes closest to the ideals of the *forme forte*. Yet with increasing globalization, where the relationship between time and space is newly defined through digital media, and where the question of local identity and an awareness of sustainability has gained in importance, "building in context" continues to move into focus.

Against this background and the overriding research strategy of this publication, the question arises: with what architectural means can the *zeitgeist* of the *forme forte* also be realized through building in existing contexts?

What role does the vertical extension in steel take on here, which in its duality of light and massive construction contrasts an inherent heterogeneity with the desired uniformity of *forme forte*?

APPARENT PHYSICAL PRESENCE OF THE MATERIAL

As early as 1849, Gottfried Semper had distinguished in his critique between the phenomenological essences of the two constructive principles of heavy and light building with iron. He saw a problem in the weak rods of iron construction deriving from lacking mass-production. However, in architecture it was a matter of satisfying the mind rather than the eyes.[3] Therefore he advised that, "Metal bars may and should be used as an economical building material in beautiful architecture, as grillwork in fences, as ornamental reticulation, but not as bearers of great masses, as the supports for a building, as the essential tone of the motif."[4] However, especially in the decades being considered here, a series of vertical extensions have been realized that ignored the warnings of Semper. Therefore it is quite noticeable that the projects discussed here employ glass actively, that is, not in an immaterial sense as in Semper's time. Computer aided research into materials at the end of the twentieth century generated a series of new possibilities for production, lending new properties to glass. Through etching, sandblasting, silk screening, printing techniques, laminating with holograms or dichroic film, this material has shown to be perceived as having a higher physical density.[5] In this way, the glass membrane gains weight in opposition to the steel skeleton, which Semper found to be inappropriate on account of the effect of the "weak bars" in "creating mass." This apparent intensification of the physical material presence had a positive effect on *forme forte*. The light building components assumed the impression of mass, approximating massive construction itself.

MULTIVALENT MATERIAL AESTHETIC

The transformation of physical density also gave the material an operative material aesthetic, just as important to a successful outcome. The multivalent expressive capacities, of which the material is now capable, is described by Terrence Riley in his text, "Light Construction," as follows: "What is mysterious about the façades is that they are sometimes transparent, sometimes translucent, sometimes opaque; mysterious, revealing, or mute, almost naturally, like a night sky shrouded in clouds, like darkness."[6] Thus it is apparent that in spite of high-tech elegance, a material can engender a "picturesque effect" as described by Heinrich Wölfflin: "[decisive] for the general feeling, are above all the cases where the light or the shadows pass over the form, that is, in contradiction to objective clarity."[7] And furthermore: "[. . .] the stable, static materiality will always be overwhelmed by the stimulation of a movement, that doesn't lie within the object [. . .]."[8] It is not "objective clarity" that determines the picturesque essence in the sense of a tectonic formation, rather the intensified atmospheric effects of the surfaces, which according to Wölfflin, produce a "hovering appearance."

The cross-reference to other disciplines, in particular painting, appears to be appropriate because, as outlined in the beginning, the façades are conceived by the architects themselves as image surfaces. This "hovering appearance" characterizes the expression of the vertical extensions as a translucent material aesthetic, such as in the case of the Bonnin House in Eichstätt (fig. 3) by Hild and K Architects, or the competition project by Diener & Diener for the Zollverein Coal Mine Ruhr Museum in Essen made of frameless cast glass (see the essay "History of Mining, Mining of History" in this publication, pp. 124–127). The "picturesque" formula also finds validity in vertical extensions with other kinds of materialities. For example, the Caixa-Forum (figs. 4, 5) in Madrid by Herzog & de Meuron with rusted Corten steel plates or the unpretentious project of BAST (figs. 6, 7) in Toulouse, where wave-like aluminum sheets reflect the surroundings, thus producing a picturesque atmosphere. This phenomenon approaches near perfection in the Elbphilharmonie in Hamburg, where fluid-like curving forms (fig. 8) imply a fictive movement.[9] In essence, these show parallels to baroque architecture, for which Wölfflin used the metaphor "events" as affirmation of a high degree of picturesque effect. By contrast, he characterized Renaissance architecture with the expression "being."[10]

RUIN-LIKE GRACE

Existing buildings often exhibit a ruin-like grace. This derives from the missing roofs and their symbolic character, as well as from the time that has etched itself into the materials. For centuries ruins have affected architectural thinking. The drawings of the Bank of England by the office of Sir John Soane may be recalled, or the numerous ruin drawings of Giovanna Battista Piranesi. With vertical extensions, this phenomenon particularly reveals itself, when the material of the added stories strongly reflects the sky, so that the structure begins to oscillate between belonging to the sky and the building. The architecture becomes a metamorphosis. Heinrich Wölfflin attributed picturesque effects to ruins: "For the same reasons, there is a picturesque beauty to ruins. The rigidity of tectonic forms is broken down, and through the crumbling of the walls [. . .] a life emerges that passes over the surfaces like a shower and shimmer."[11]

It becomes clear that the picturesque medium unifies the contrasting materiality of the base structure and the vertical addition with its "veil." A phenomenological effect establishes itself, which on the second view has more layers than assumed, in accordance with the canon of *forme forte*. When Jacques Herzog speaks of the aluminum objects by Judd in Marfa, Texas (fig. 9), which he sees as being represented by *Untitled (Six Cold Rolled Steel Boxes)*, he lauds their effect within the exhibition context: "The works have the effect of a totality, almost like a metallic space that continually changes appearance, which with its varied light and reflective effects stands in stark contrast to the raw landscape outside. In the usual gallery or museum context, the same works often have a somewhat decorative effect."[12] That the wild landscape of Texas says more to him than the white cube, is probably due

3

4

5

6

7

REDISCOVERY OF METAMORPHOSIS   118

to the picturesque presence of the landscape. For the reflective cube, which is also subject to the picturesque, creates a "totality" with the context, although in the same breath Herzog speaks of a "stark contrast." This contrast is comparable to the massive and light construction of the examples mentioned here, which in spite of different identities find unity through the picturesque.

LIMITS OF PHYSICALITY

If we leave the level of material aesthetics, then we realize that the specific factors related to vertical extensions, in particular load bearing, are conducive to *forme forte*. Avoiding projections and recesses as an appropriate response to this premise leads to a simple form. In addition, the functional pragmatism of industrial building is often expressed in simple plan figures, which also satisfy the principles of *forme forte*. It results in simple volumes, which suppress every tectonic expression, thus bestowing an even greater role on the edges of the volume. They distinguish the physical form from its surroundings.[13] The reduction of form gives them an extraordinary power, which is able to hold the layered coexistence of two heterogenous material worlds together in a *forme forte*. This phenomenological configuration is witnessed by the Elbphilharmonie, where its bold power is sufficient to integrate the full-height interstice between base and addition (fig. 10).

The missing eave line, which often contributes to an ambiguity between the existing and the vertical extension, is compensated through a technologically determined change of material quality in this kind of vertical extension. In this way it shows that this strategy for adding stories can only be complimented by the technological material developments of this era. These open up the possibility of vertical extension without the ambiguous boundary of the eave line, so that the two symbiotic "connectors" tend towards a unified whole—the simple and powerful form.

The technological material developments of our time occur much more quickly than in the past. This condition, among others, may be traced back to increasing digitization. A comparison of the Salamander Shoe Factory of 1927 (see the essay "Dressed in an Old Coat" in this publication, pp. 40-43) with the Elbphilharmonie illustrates precisely the differing architectural requirements for this change in building concepts. The former continues with the same materiality, from the base structure to the vertical extension. The latter manifests its expression through two diametric material entities. Within contemporary vertical extensions, the gap between the existing and new stories continues to expand further in respect to material identity. In particular, if technological material progress is to be economically advantageous, this aspect of the architectural project is an essential determinant. As explained in respect to the "picturesque," the new technological material possibilities at the same time also expand the spectrum in relation to existing materialities. Against this background, it is clear that construction within existing building fabric, which due to its alleged lack of expressiveness long stood in the shadows of new construction, now has the capacity to qualify for monumentality.

119

8

9

10

Forme forte as a means of cohesion between old and new, here for example the Elbphilharmonie in Hamburg by Herzog & de Meuron, 2017.

REDISCOVERY OF METAMORPHOSIS

1 Martin Steinmann, *Martin Steinmann – Forme forte: Schriften 1972–2002* (Basel: 2003), p. 197.
2 See Philip Ursprung, *Herzog & de Meuron: Naturgeschichte* (Zurich: 2002), p. 13
3 Gottfried Semper, "Eisenkonstruktionen" (1849), in idem, *Materialästhetik: Quellentexte zu Kunst, Design und Architektur,* Dietmar Rübe, et al., eds. (Berlin: 2005), p. 62.
4 Ibid.
5 See Christian Schittich, "Die Glasarchitektur von der Moderne bis zur Gegenwart," in idem, *Glasbau-Atlas,* (Basel: 2006), p. 42.
6 Terence Riley, "Light Construction", in *Arch+,* 129/130 (1995): *Herzog & de Meuron. Minimalismus und Ornament,* p. 109, cited in *Arch+,* 144/145 (1998): *Kommende Transparenz,* p. 99.
7 Heinrich Wölfflin, *Kunstgeschichtliche Grundbegriffe. Das Problem der Stilentwicklung in der neueren Kunst,* 19th ed. (Basel: 2004), p. 41.
8 Ibid., p. 39.
9 While the competition project was still planned with a vertical extension, in further project development the former cocoa warehouse could not be adapted to the increasingly complex usage, despite the relatively small structural module. As a result, the core of the warehouse was removed so that a completely new structure could be erected within the old brick façades of the warehouse. See Daniel Kurz, "Schweben als Kraftakt. Zum statischen System der Elbphilharmonie," in *Werk, Bauen + Wohnen,* 104, no. 6 (2017), p. 51. Nevertheless, the image of the story addition was retained. The CaixaForum in Madrid is comparable, which is why it is included in this analysis as a case study for phenomenological perception.
10 See Wölfflin, *Kunstgeschichtliche Grundbegriffe* (see note 7), p. 22.
11 Ibid., p. 39.
12 Jacques Herzog and Pierre de Meuron, "Transformation und Verfremdung," in Ursprung, *Herzog & de Meuron* (see note 2), p. 87.
13 See Rudolf Arnheim, *Kunst und Sehen: Eine Psychologie des schöpferischen Auges,* 3rd ed. (Berlin/New York: 2000), p. 50.

REDISCOVERY OF METAMORPHOSIS 122

History of Mining, Mining of History

The Design for the Reconstruction of the Zollverein Coal Mine, Shaft XII
   Jürg Conzett and Roger Diener

Already after its completion, the mining facility of central Shaft XII of the Zollverein Coal Mine was considered to be a prime example of a successful collaboration between engineer and architect. The design by Fritz Schupp and Martin Kremmer, with the engineering office of F. Zoepke was "an event that outshined everything in the history" of Ruhr-Area coal mining.[1] This architectural and technological masterwork was thought to be trailblazing in terms of objective, functional industrial construction, and an important example of the New Objectivity. It was proof, according to architect Fritz Schupp, that only a collaborative work between an engineer and an architect, "leads to a mutual enhancement of capabilities."[2]

Erected from 1928 to 1932, this facility was the largest of its kind in the world in its time, with a 12,000 ton daily capacity, and was praised as "not only the most beautiful coal mine in the Ruhr Area, but also the most modern in Germany, indeed in Europe, or even the entire world."[3] (fig. 1) Industry and its powerful buildings, according to the architects, should no longer be, "a disturbing element in our city and landscape, rather a symbol of work, an urban monument, which every citizen should point out to tourists with at least as much pride as public buildings."[4]

Following its closure on December 23, 1986, and the subsequent years of uncertainty, the reconstruction process for this "cathedral of the Ruhr Area" began with its boiler house, which was to be rebuilt as the location for the North Rhine Westphalia Design Center. Important buildings are situated by the entrance to the coalmine facing the city. Most of the initial renovation and repurposing was carried out in this section. Behind it lies an axis of production with a series of buildings and silos moving the coal, all expressively interconnected with overhead conveyors. The highlight of this section is the coal washery, a towering machine with conveyor belts in the middle of a railyard, symbolizing the production and transport of the coal. Schupp and Kremmer placed the striking headframe at the pivotal point between the two sections.

PROPOSAL FOR THE RESTRUCTURING
OF THE FACILITY BY SCHUPP, KREMMER,
AND ZOEPKE

For the reuse of the coal mine closed in 1986, a competition was held in 1999 within a framework that would award multiple commissions.[5] The project by Diener & Diener Architects in collaboration with the engineer Jürg Conzett was awarded the first prize, and recommended for realization.[6] The design proposal thematized the production axis of the Zollverein Coal Mine Shaft XII: the restoration of the tracks, the coal washery, and the rail station, and in addition the new Ruhr Museum and a design school. The coalmine was incorporated within the Emscher Landscape Park in the Northern Ruhr Area, a regional cooperation in connection with the Emscher Park Building Exhibition. It united within a new park type the existing objects of the preindustrial cultural landscape, regional green areas designated since 1920, as well as parts of the postindustrial mining landscape of the Ruhr Area.

The project for the infrastructure of the coalmine was connected to the Ruhr Museum in terms of content. Along with other flagships, this was to be a building block within the architectural vision for the Zollverein Coal Mine, where in future the development of the Ruhr Area was to be observed, questioned, and represented.

The project for the coal washery link to the rail station in the middle of the railyard. Container-like exhibition storage units, some located off track, some on, were to display part of the collection of the Ruhr Museum. The logistics of the museum and the design school re-enlivened the combination of delivery, storage, and freight train station, and allowed one to imagine the 800 tons of coal that were transferred here on an hourly basis when the coal mine was operational.

The headframe, shaft hall, cart return, and coal washery were the symbols of the coal refinement process in Shaft XII of the Zollverein Coal Mine. Particularly on a first visit, the enormous power and energy of this great technical mining operation within the framework of rational construction becomes clear. The various overhead conveyors held these buildings and machines together in a singular whole. This production complex developed independently from the significant urban buildings facing the shopping street, which are structurally rigorous but aesthetically constructed. In spite of their architectonic relationship, the two ensembles could not be more different: facing the city, the classical elegant complex with court of honor, visual axis, and freestanding buildings; behind it the towering buildings carrying coal, whose form was determined by their mechanical functions (fig. 2).

The key witness to the inseparably connected series of buildings, spaces, and machines for the refinement of the raw material was the coal washery. How could this simple and self-evident continuum, to which Schupp and Kremmer gave a unique expression, be maintained in spite of, and yet in harmony with, its new uses? The coal washery's intended purpose was to create an awareness of the production processes; therefore, its spatial sequence was not to be changed.

As a result of this consideration, the now defunct halls of the coal washery were located underneath, and permanently and purely connected to a museum realized above in the form of a vertical extension. In the coal washery, time appears to have come to a sudden standstill. For the visitor, the tour of the building was about experiencing the coal and the machinery—an experience that remained immediate, free from intervening didactic or interpretative layers. The expansion into a museum treated the coal washery as an original architectural, urban, or topographical element, which entered into a simultaneous relationship with the other buildings, including all of the machinery. For the Ruhr Museum exhibitions, new spaces were created, a kind of Ruhr Deck, like the deck of a ship. Had they had been housed *within* the work halls of the coal washery, then that the exhibition objects probably would have lost their magic for all times. The dialogue between the exhibition materials and the coal mining machinery would only have been satisfactory in this location for the short term. The solution chosen by the design museum a few years earlier, of displaying the old equipment like stage set decorations, was not to be repeated.

In this design, the new museum and the design school, with a floor area of 13,200 square meters on three levels, would have been primarily located above the great hall of the coal washery (fig. 6). The intention was to allow the historic and current state of the place to be meaningfully perceived, as the visitor moves upwards above the old lifting facilities. From the first opening days of the museum, the well-equipped halls of the coal washery below give the impression that the workers had just gone home. The vertical connection in this scenario awakened a sense of how the coal was carried up from the depths into the coal washery, in order to be sorted, washed, and then directed through chutes into the carts.

The view thus revealed by the museum within its coalfield, the working sphere of the museum, reflects its cultural mission. The visitor was not to experience the exhibitions and installations as static presentations, which displace the monument, but rather as the working products of the observation of processes that continue to develop.

VERTICAL EXTENSION AS
A MEANS OF REINFORCEMENT

In architectural history, the best vertical extensions facilitate the heightening of the quality of monumental buildings, without diminishing the effect of the original fabric. The architectural expression of such extensions is rich in associations, without the new effacing the boundary with the existing building. The Villa Farnese in Caprarola is an excellent example of this. Erected in about 1500 as a fortress with a pentagonal plan, in 1560 following plans by Giacomo Barozzi da Vignola two stories were added above the bastion to elevate it to a summer residence. The vertical extension above the coal washery followed the same principles. The new stories were placed exactly above the existing building volume. The main building section was again the highest elevation.

A metal scaffold hangs in front of the supporting steel structure of the coal washery by Schupp and Kremmer, which is filled-in with brick and window bands.[7] It formed a thin skin that didn't make the powerful, cubic form of the coal washery appear to be heavy. The relatively smooth base and the light shaft of the building appear almost transparent. Even the two corner elements in the main section lie flush with the plane of the façade; for the extension, the two corner elements became determining architectonic spatial forms. In the remaining sections as well, the extension was to continue every theme within the existing building. The fragility of the façade skin was enhanced through translucency in the vertical extension.

Since the closure of the coalmine, disconcerting corrosion damage has appeared on the framework and on the steel rebars in the concrete. Some of the columns in the coal washery showed concrete spalls and exposed rebars. Reports revealed the necessity for building and structural measures for the preservation of the coal washery. The synergistic project for the vertical extension at the same time involved the restoration of the coal washery. The waste heat produced by the museum was to stabilize the corrosion process in the interior of the machine hall, without having to thermally insulate the outer shell of the coal washery. The structural reinforcements that were necessary in order to maintain the coal washery long term, and to support the vertical extension, were the determining factors for the concept.

REDISCOVERY OF METAMORPHOSIS

With a height of up to 17.3 meters the coal washery is a powerful, massive building. Within it are several floors of steel construction. The uppermost story is a hall spanned by double-hinged frames. The framing bars follow the contour of the lightly double-pitched roof (fig. 5). For the vertical extension, as per the project proposal the framing action would literally be stood on its head.

Triangular rods were screwed onto the surface of the double-pitched roof, which carry the lowest level of the museum (the existing copper-alloy steel can no longer be welded today). These triangular rods merge together into new vertical framing elements extending above. The higher floor decks act as tension elements, which push the overhead framework outwards as far as possible, so that the bending moment in the existing vertical framing elements disappears. Thus reserve capacity is freed up in the existing steel framework, which allows the added stories to be placed atop the old steel construction without having to reinforce it (figs. 3, 4). The prerequisite for this is that the new floor decks are stabilized against horizontal effects through the new vertical circulation cores, so that the existing frame only receives vertical forces.

In spite of, and thanks to, the upward extension of the gantry supports, the original concrete roof could be kept and the interior space be preserved in its original state.

In this approach, the principles of Schupp and Kremmer, the history of the monument, and its expression appear to be seamlessly integrated with one another in order to maintain the original power of the coal washery to the utmost extent. As a unique witness to the inseparable, interconnected relationship of spaces and machines, architecture and structural engineering in combination, this project renders the presence of the original structure by a vertical extension in steel.[8]

1 Walter Buschmann, "Zeche und Kokerei Zollverein: Form, Sinn, Herkunft und Verarbeitung," in Udo Mainzer (ed.), *Zeche und Kokerei Zollverein: Das Weltkulturerbe* (Worms: 2006), pp. 47–76, here p. 48.

2 "Fritz Schupp: Bemerkungen des Architekten," in F. Zoepke, "Geschweisste Konstruktionen bei den Übertagebauten einer Grossschachtanlage," in *Der Bauingenieur* 13, no. 21/22 (1932), pp. 297–302, here p. 297.

3 *Die Steinkohlebergwerke der Vereinigte Stahlwerke AG, Zollverein,* vol. 1 (Essen: 1935), p. 54.

4 Fritz Schupp, "Architekt gegen oder und Ingenieur," in *Der Industriebau: Monatsschrift für die künstlerische und technische Förderung aller Gebiete industrieller Bauten, einschliesslich aller Ingenieurbauten, sowie der gesamten Fortschritte der Technik* 20, no. 5 (1929), pp. 174–180, here pp. 179–180.

5 Five offices were commissioned to prepare project proposals: Böll & Krabel, Essen; Jürg Steiner, Berlin; Peter Kulka, Cologne; Allmann, Sattler, Wappner of Munich; Diener & Diener, Basel.

6 See Irma Noseda, "Aufstockung als Signal der neuen Nutzung: Das Ruhrmuseum-Projekt von Diener & Diener und Jürg Conzett," in *Werk, Bauen + Wohnen* 87, no. 5 (2000), pp. 42–47.

7 A journal article on the steel construction was written by the designers: F. Zoepke and Fritz Schupp, "Geschweisste Konstruktionen bei den Übertagebauten einer Grossschachtanlage" (see note 2).

8 Editor's note: In the end, the fear that the added stories could overwhelm the headframe and thus endanger the application for inclusion in the UNESCO cultural heritage list led to the development of another project under the direction of Rem Kohlhaas.

1

The vertical addition of frameless cast glass extends the coal washery with respect to the principles of construction and the materials inherent in the building. Thus the only change is in height, while the geometric contour remains. The new museum on the roof of the coal washery is visibly different, but not emphasized.

REDISCOVERY OF METAMORPHOSIS   128

2

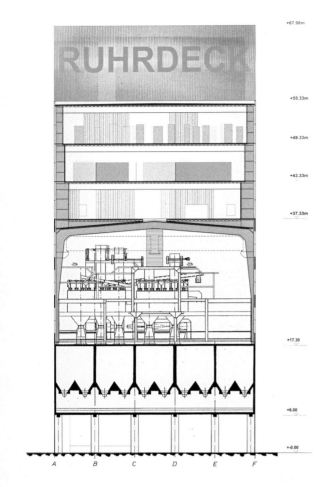
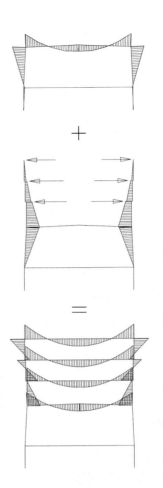

3
4

5

REDISCOVERY OF METAMORPHOSIS 130

6

3,4 Only by reiterating the framing effect can the vertical addition be achieved without having to reinforce the old steel construction.
5   In the museum interior, in the abandoned halls of the coal washery, time appears to have come to a sudden stop. For the visitor, the experience of the building, the coal, and the machinery is truly immediate, without didactic or interpretive interventions.
An extension of a monument only makes sense when it enriches it as an architectural, urbanistic, or topographic element.

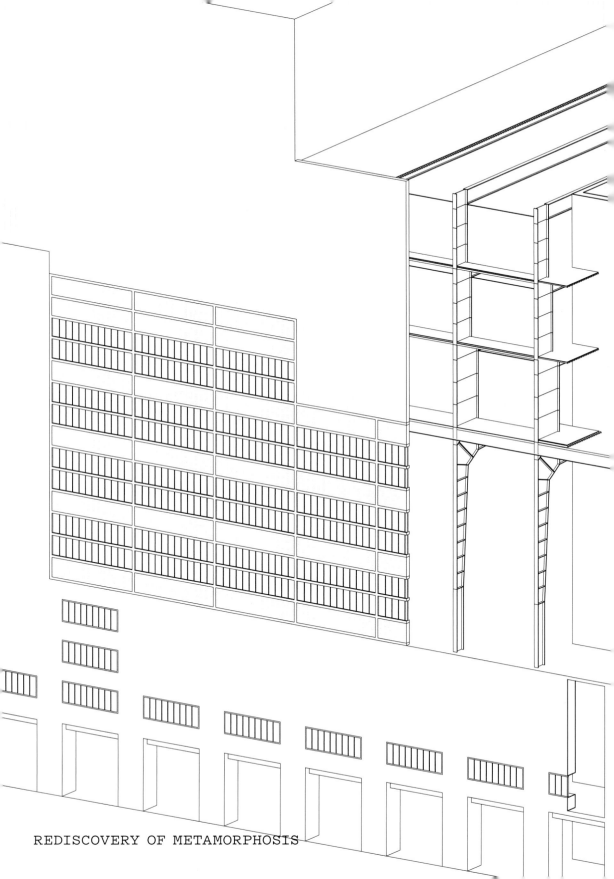

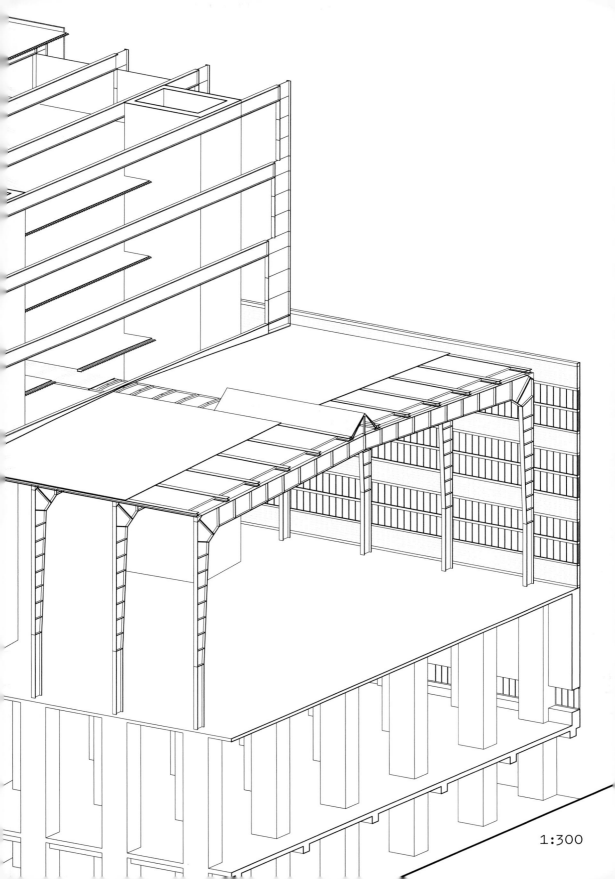

1:300

HOW TO BUILD ON?

Ways towards Ambiguity and Multivalence

Astrid Staufer   p. 136

On the New Potentials of Steel Construction

Patric Fischli-Boson   p. 156

Ways towards Ambiguity and Multivalence

Astrid Staufer

This publication recounts the eventful history of vertical extensions during the eras of the proto-modern, the modern, and the postmodern. An effect of the genre of science-fiction films is that every generation projects its fears and hopes onto the future, the spaceship, and the infinity of outer space. In a similar manner, the vertical extensions that seem to hover over architecture like an ever-changing "sky-dome" also engender such projections. However, what perspectives and potentials may we expect today from the genre of vertical extensions, beyond the choice of material?

VERTICAL EXTENSION AS SOCIAL PROJECTION MODEL

"We behave similarly towards the existing. The more we comprehend it, the less we have to confront it, and the easier it is to understand our decisions as the extension of a continuum. A rebuild is more interesting than a new build—because in principle everything is a rebuild." Hermann Czech (1989).[1]

While a perusal of the history of vertical extensions reveals an impressive palette of ideologically nourished strategies and bold experiments with effects, the harvest of contemporary examples since the turn of the millennium nevertheless appears to be rather sobering. This is also apparent in an edition of *Werk, Bauen + Wohnen* from early 2017, with the title, "Vertical Extensions—City at Eave Height," which presented a cross section through the current state of the genre.[2] A broad spectrum of predominately form-oriented themes reflected the uncertainty of a society in transformation, whose architectural vocabulary has entered a mannerist phase following decades of the decline of a canon. The resulting pluralism oscillates between sober reserve and ambitious acts of liberation. This reveals that the discipline of vertical extensions deals with a highly challenging situation, with its dizzying range of social, urbanistic, architectonic, normative, constructive, and technical requirements that must be brought together into a synthesis; otherwise these can open up particular abysses. The vertical extension always attaches itself to that which exists: the existing city, in which the architecture of the object is manifested. As a new whole, the consolidation of the existing with its additions must always be better than what is already there. "In sum," continues Czech, "old construction

is superior to new construction *ex definitione*: by the inimitable character of ageing."[3]

In dealing with this challenge, each era has developed its own strategy in answer to the questions that shape it. Within the proto-modern as a link between epochs, the theme of vertical extensions is a pragmatic starting point for a renewed building tradition; the conservation of resources unceremoniously produced an expanded tectonic, without thematizing the evidence of this temporal shift. The tectonic domesticated everything, even the changing proportions of the building mass.[4] Within the modern, by contrast, vertical extensions almost completely disappeared. Modernism favored building on green fields, and distanced itself from consideration of the existing context. This was only renewed in postwar modernism, primarily in connection with the discussion of the newly perceived relationship of *antico e moderno* in Italian reconstruction, where the treatment of the so-called pre-existing was debated, that is, an interest in confronting the existing: in this case, vertical extensions were always understood as a (critical) commentary on this, and the relationship between existing and addition was often dramatically reversed.[5] As a consequence of the utopias of the 1960s and 1970s,[6] within the deconstructivism of the 1980s this increasingly dissolves into an oppositional figure, in which the addition as a futuristic construct frees itself from the stoniness of the pre-existing.[7] Finally, at the turn of the millennium, a group focused on abstract art revisited the vertical extension in a complementary relationship to the existing, which didn't seek identity through form but rather through contrasting materiality, as facilitated by new technologies.[8]

And today? What may we learn from history? At least one point appears to emerge: the more social, the more political the mission of the time, then the more interesting the results in retrospect. Can a critical review motivate us

1 Cross section as a reflection of the social hierarchy: drawing "Cinq étages du monde parisien" by Charles Bertall in *Le Diable à Paris,* vol. 2 (Paris: 1846).

HOW TO BUILD ON? 138

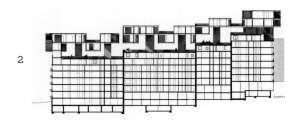

2 Vertical extension as a collective project: Student project by Giulia Altarelli and Elsa Beniada for the course "Mon aire—mon repos" in Lausanne, Atelier Staufer & Hasler, EPFL LABEX 2009.

3, 4 An extension as part of both city street planning and the collective urban space high above the ground: vertical extension on Curtain Road in London by Duggan Morris Architects, 2010.

to understand the vertical extension not as an exclusively individual and formal problem, but once again as a sociopolitical one?

Today to whom does this very precious space under the sky belong, where earlier students and servants dwelled, yet which now harbors essential further densification potential? In fact, in relation to the sectional hierarchy a transformation has taken place. In the late nineteenth century the *piano nobile,* as the tallest floor that was also easily accessible by foot, was located on the second floor (above or below the mezzanine), from where one waved from the balcony overlooking the street at the coaches passing by. However, today the so-called lower social strata live there, closer to the ground near the motorized traffic.[9] In the airy heights the most expensive apartments, served by elevators, tower above the city as desirable objects of speculative interest. It is not surprising that students, far removed from economic feasibility, think about how this sky space could have its elite privacy stripped away and be made accessible to a collective—if not the public then at least the occupants and users of the house.[10] Approaches to this kind of multiple-reading are illustrated by Duggan Morris's project on Curtain Road in London (2010), that reveals its relationship to the orderly urban streetscape on the one side, and on the other side to a collective exterior space over the roofs of the city. The façade composition of the vertical extension on the street side continues the existing order of the pilasters in the form of elements and materials in a very abstract manner, following the rhythm of the streetscape despite its new materiality. However, by contrast on the courtyard side of the roof level a staggered volume with lightwells and exterior spaces comes into free play. Within the fragmented context of the greater metropolitan area lying beyond the courtyard structure, it gives the occupants a second sense of belonging to a collective space over the roofscape.

VERTICAL EXTENSIONS AS URBAN DENSIFICATION STRATEGY

"That which exists is the city. It is stronger than anything that one can do as opposed to its own invention. Instead of building a well-planned world, we discover a powerful mass, which through the insertion of small things we can only change, defamiliarize, reinterpret, perhaps steer. But as with nature, this mass is much more an object of recognition than of change."[11]
Herman Czech (1973)

Through its historic urban densification strategies, Geneva shows the potential for an overall interconnection of vertical extensions within the *Stadtkrone* [city crown], if indeed initially only to a limited degree.[12] Ideally the city will expand itself not only as a coincidental series of individual vertical objects, but rather unify its connection to the sky in the horizontal direction as well, through a dynamic crown that bestows identity. When such processes have already begun, through which an entire quarter comes under the control of one hand—similar to the case of the harbor complex canal in Wijnegem (BE), where existing packing and storage houses are being remodeled into a commercial, office, and apartment complex—it makes the double reading of the city in both the vertical and horizontal direction easier to realize. Even if the project by Coussée & Goris (2007–2016) with its steel cranes set on existing brick buildings appears somewhat didactic (and one would expect something more than profane luxury apartments behind the steel spatial layers), it does indeed illustrate the potential for a rhythmic, hovering city crown, that lends a new presence to the existing.

A more regulated approach is required for urbanistic aims in the context of individual initiatives, where densification guidelines and masterplans must ensure urban order. Such is the case with the former Zollfreilager [bonded warehouse] in Zurich, built in the 1930s by Pfleghard & Häfelli on a greenfield site, recently transformed through a tedious process by Meili Peter architects from a free warehouse area into a new apartment complex with 1,000 rental units at a new urban scale (2004–2016). Here the city overtook the periphery in great strides. The masterplan directs the dramaturgy of height and open space, and allows for building masses with between five and eight stories, as well as towers, requiring a "particular quality" across the building site, as ensured by the competition.[13] The notable achievement of the vertical extension realized here, is that the existing buildings were made to appear at the same time as part of the rescaled site. Their historical presence was also made legible in the individual objects through a cleverly composed reiterative shape.

The continuous "rising up" of the urban scale in the constantly expanding highrise districts mentioned above also characterizes Christian Kerez's proposal for the ewz site Herdern in Zurich-West (2016), commissioned by the City of Zurich. For operational reasons, the retention of the existing substation was required. In order to reinforce the axis along the improved Pfingstweidstrasse, already lined with high-rises, it will be double-loaded: on the one side with a four-story addition with direct load transfer, on the other with a detached eight-story building structure elevated above it. An exoskeleton, i. e., an external support structure, carries the loads freely on all four sides, forming a powerful high-rise slab. Through this double-operation a spectacular and at the same time hybrid expression is produced, which according to the jury report, "would be suited to an industrial services operation."[14] At the same time, this new "construct" also entered into

HOW TO BUILD ON?

an intensive dialog with the architecture of the neighboring Migros high-rise slab, and the Toni-Areal across from it. Single-story existing buildings thus become the generator of a building configuration, which is embodied and structurally incorporated within the gradually increasing height of the city.

VERTICAL EXTENSION FROM WITHIN

> "Reuse and rebuilding are a reinterpretation of the existing building stock, thus opening us up to ambiguity and and multivalence. Space and building arise from varied and often contradictory thought processes; their perceptible network forms the 'aesthetic information density.' Historic multilayering is the model for others: spatial multilayering more or less the superimposition of coincident (or even simulated) spatial concepts."[15]
> Hermann Czech (1977)

The late-nineteenth-century city, protected by building and district preservation laws, occupies large areas of Europe's inner cities. Above its eaves, it offers a quantitatively modest, yet qualitatively attractive potential for densification, owing to its privileged location. A research study conducted over the course of several years by the Institute of Constructive Design at the ZHAW investigated strategies for the "reclamation of cold [unused] roofs"[16]—a factor which in the early 1990s was only reflected in Zurich laws through a vague specification of "neighborhood compatibility."[17]

Within the framework of fundamental research for the preparation of new guidelines for the City of Zurich, when analyzing existing legislation the guidelines were understood to have some "maneuvering room." The regulations concerning the number of stories had to be complied with, but with regard to dormers and roof insertions they were open to interpretation in respect to the overall effect. Comparative montages show how, when respecting given laws, the street space is not weakened by intermittent volumetric protrusions and accentuations of the

5

6

HOW TO BUILD ON? 142

5   A continuous crown above the city: conversion and extension project by Coussée & Goris architecten am Kanaal, Wijnegem (Belgium), 2007–2016, model study.
6   Transformation on a new urban scale: building addition and densification of the former Zollfreilager by Pfleghard & Haefeli from the 1930s to realize the new residential development Freilager in Zurich Albisrieden. Meili, Peter Architekten, 2004–2016 (master plan, entire site, conversion and addition of existing buildings).
7, 8 Materialization of the progressive rising up of the city: double story addition model with direct load transfer as well as load transfer via exoskeleton above the existing substructure. Contribution by Christian Kerez for the commissioned study for the ewz site Herdern in Zurich-West, 2016; structural model and site model.

roof mass above the eaves, rather it can even be enhanced. "In the context of the perimeter block development", states Patric Furrer (an academic collaborator in the research team noted above) in a conversation published in *Werk, Bauen + Wohnen,* "the eave line is an element that binds, but for the individual house it is an element that separates. But it should not only separate, rather at exactly this point it must establish a relationship between the proportions of the façade and those of the addition. A vertical extension is thus successful when it sets up a relationship, an ambiguity between the above and below."[18] Where the scope for design on the exterior is restricted due to historic preservation requirements, one can still be more creative within the interior. This gives room for the development of additional domestic qualities: the possibility of sun exposure and views of the sky enriches the urban-living repertoire with new lighting and spatial situations, whether through "mega-dormers," through openings directly at the intersection of wall and roof, or through recesses or inset courts.

In his own roof extension on Günthergasse in Vienna (2011), Hermann Czech demonstrates with a type of triple dormer window how the reinterpretation of a mansard roof towering above the city can contribute to architectural as well as spatial ambiguity. On the exterior this hybrid dormer interacts with the superstructures, domes, and decorative gables of its nineteenth-century neighbors. On the interior, it creates a highly complex spatial and lighting situation by combining a protruding dormer window with a generous rectangular opening, additionally providing it with a peephole focused on the distant view of the Votivkirche over the adjoining inset terrace. "The projected incision in the roof," Czech explains in his project description, "creates a further 'backdrop' element behind the historicist ornamental gable parallel to the front of the house. In this way,

9

10

Research project at the Institute of Constructive Design (IKE) at ZHAW concerning the development of the cold roofs of perimeter blocks in the city of Zurich. Exploration of densification and planning potential above the eaves, in keeping with neighborhood compatibility requirements. Model studies and photo collages were used for this purpose.

the two building tendencies become clearer. The design strives for a more informative, rather than coarser, perception of detail."[19]

The building regulations did not allow for two roof stories, but indeed for a gallery. This provided the opportunity for the picturesque formation of a complex, flowing spatial figure moving in all directions, that "makes those spaces conceivable," according to Czech in one of his theoretical texts,

11

12

13

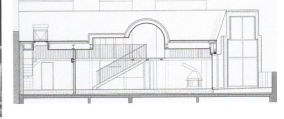

Architectural and spatial ambiguity above the *Gründerzeit*-era city: triple dormer in the attic conversion by Hermann Czech on Vienna's Günthergasse, 2011.

"whose effect is not based on their architectural form, but on their lighting conditions. Not only would such architecture affect that which the experience already depends upon most [. . .], it would also be able to change its effects, without having to touch the material."[20] Czech's working plans also demonstrate the advantages of steel construction for roof additions where, due to the given building sections, the structural capacity must be maximally optimized for the benefit of space gain, and above all for the spatial experience.

VERTICAL EXTENSIONS AS PART OF A SERIES OF DECISIONS

> "The characteristic feature of rebuilding—we now return to architectural design—derives from the fact that decisions are already given. Once you realize that each design process represents a series of decisions, in which later decisions are determined by earlier ones, it then makes no difference whether the earlier decisions were your own or someone else's. Each design process entails decisions, which following subsequent thinking must either be accepted or overturned. [. . .] Whoever wants to communicate new thoughts cannot employ a new language at the same time."[21]
> Hermann Czech (1989)

The question of what constitutes the correct decision in the "series of decisions" described by Czech will be pursued through a set of contemporary case studies that transform "earlier decisions" into their own, thus making use of a "new language." This strategy can have very different effects.

For the 2001 conversion of an exposed concrete building by the SIA Hochhaus architect Hans von Meyenburg from 1970 in Zurich Altstetten, the architects Romero & Schäfle decided on a complete reinterpretation.[22] The five-story existing building, with its striking continuous banding and strips of windows ordered in the manner typical of the time, was taken back to the underlying construction. A two-story vertical extension was added: of lightweight construction (steel frame with Holorib sheet-metal decking), entirely re-clad and reinterpreted as an elegant and distinctly planar "new building volume." Even the scrutinizing, practiced gaze of the observer will become lost among the differentiated floor heights, because the mass of the over-height, existing attic floor was transferred onto the vertical extension, thus literally veiling the incision point of the operation. "It was first Loos," wrote Czech in "Der Umbau," "who could write the story of the poor rich man that told us that a dwelling, a house, must continue to live through its user, and withstand the decisions of a different taste, meaning a different ethic." He certainly did not mean this in a moralist sense, for as Andreas Vass explained in his commentary on Czech's essay, rebuilding extends to, "everything existing, from the material to immaterial, to the presence of concepts formulated by others or even by ourselves. It forms the brackets, within which the dialectic between preservation, alteration, and destruction is set in motion each time. The series of decisions by others or ourselves falls within the existing, which is absorbed within a design totality, without deriving ideological guidelines from this."[23]

A contrary position to this attitude of concealment can be seen in the vertical extension projects of the Danish office BIG for the rebuilding of transport facility in Münchenstein (2016), and the guesthouse of the ETH Science City by llg Santer on Zurich's Hönggerberg (project 2007).[24] They highlight the unique, even sculptural character of the vertical extension in contrast to the existing. While the guesthouse searches for more of a complementary, or balanced and augmenting relationship, the project by BIG stands in a contrasting relationship to it. In their commentary "Oben ist anders" [Up above Is Different] in *Werk, Bauen + Wohnen* likewise identifies this contrast: "Horizontal lightness above solemn heaviness." Yet in the mediation of the two geometries it "grates:" this is above all the fault of the great building depth to be mastered, and the intention of allowing a longer façade composition to result. However, the interfaces between the different geometries of the existing and the vertical extension would inevitably require, "compromises when carrying the coherent overall conception down to the next level of detail."[25]

In contrast to this, the unfortunately not (yet) realized project of llg Santer (with a structural concept by Lüchinger + Meyer)

14

15

Erased traces: vertical extension and transformation of the exposed-concrete building by Hans von Meyenburg (1970), by Romero & Schäfle into new offices for Helvetia, Zurich Altstetten, 2001.

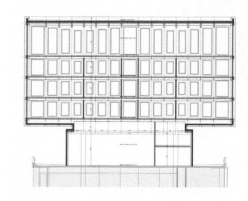

draws its entire strength from the constructive demands that it imposes upon itself. It complements the laboratory by Albert H. Steiner (1965)—its added technical installations giving it a fragmented appearance today—with a composed "head" that looks out across the open landscape via an intermediary "neck." The cleverly conceived steel structure of the vertical extension is made possible by the massive longitudinal projection of the Vierendeel trusses. On the interior the load distribution is revealed, while on the exterior a curtain wall of steel profiles covers the truss structure. Thus, this project presents an innovative contribution to multi-story steel construction, while delivering an elegantly translated commentary on the technological orientation of the existing architecture.

Shaped more by sculptural approaches, yet anchored in extensive sociological studies, the master's project of ETH diploma student Ricardo Joss engages with the densification of the Talbächli cooperative housing project at the Letzigraben in Zurich (Prof. Tom Emerson, ETH Zurich, 2016).

16 Oppositional figure: transformation and vertical extension of the transit warehouse in Münchenstein by Bjarke Ingels Group (BIG), 2016.
17 Detail of the northwest corner of the former transit warehouse, bonded warehouse Dreispitz, BIG, 2016.
18 Laboratory building by Albert H. Steiner, 1965, ETH Zürich Hönggerberg.
19 Complementation: added guest house at Science City ETH by Ilg Santer, competition project, 2007.
20 Section drawing of the steel Vierendeel trusses by Dr. Lüchinger + Meyer, Zurich.

21

22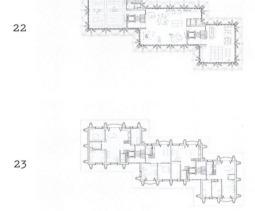

24

23

Densification with new dwellings for the Talbächli cooperative housing project in Zurich: diploma project of Ricardo Joss, Chair of Tom Emerson, ETHZ, 2016.

Because the existing stock functions well despite limited deficiencies, Joss posed the question of whether a building without lifts that steps down a cliff and has three split-levels could be redesigned with new kinds of living space: "How can a diverse spatial offering be created in addition to dwelling? [. . .] The liveliness, potential usages, and diversity of this housing project led me to this choice."[26] Even if the retention of less architecturally valuable existing stock appears to be scarcely realistic under current economic conditions, it nevertheless contains a rich source from which themes may be derived. Through the search for "maximum diversity," the material for a customized building configuration was created based on an analysis of communal life. In a similar manner to Kerez, the problem of carrying a load over an existing building was resolved through a structural envelope that extended over buttressing à la Torre Velasca, in order to incorporate more living area.[27] The seam between old and new was coherently developed as a communal level, and the existing stairways supplemented with an elevator. In this manner, all of the themes that must stand up to the realities of vertical extensions were thus engaged.

THE VERTICAL EXTENSION AS CREATOR OF AMBIGUITY AND MULTIVALENCE

"Rebuilding is not just a matter of subduing new construction through compromises, rather the elements of the old building with its changes join with the newly created elements in a new unity, representing a fully valid work."[28]
Hermann Czech (1989)

With this student project that is interconnected on many levels, we already have come somewhat closer to the concluding question of the ideals and potentials of vertical extensions. From our perspective, how can the single yet highly challenging goal of "multi-layered, multivalent unity" be achieved within the discipline of vertical extensions? Even more so than within architecture in general, it is defined by being simultaneously included within multiple epistemes: urban design, history, construction, space, and, above all, the life that takes place therein. Out of this grows the specific expression that makes the existing readable as part of the "series of decisions," and touches us as a new unity, like two lovers who have found one another. It should not only be the case that one, the new, emerges from the old; much more than this, the new enriches the old and increases its value, not only making it larger, but also stronger, and more sublime.

Through this quest, many projects were produced in a course led by ETH professor Peter Märkli, who in 2002–2003 dedicated himself to theme of vertical extensions at Schaffhauserplatz in Zurich.[29] There the construction enhanced the existing stock where it already had strengths, and covered over its weaknesses, while setting what was there within a new, emphatic light. Thanks to the new construction the house obtains new status in respect to its manifold, multivalent sense of belonging. This is what makes the discipline of vertical extensions so demanding. Through vertical extension, the rebuild does not simply remain a rebuild, for it sets new standards, it becomes the litmus paper, the model for the rebuilding of the city.

Through his own work as well, Peter Märkli has made an impact on the rebuilding of the city, in this way opening up a long-standing debate as to what historic preservation means today. His project for a vertical extension to the Old Stock Exchange on Bahnhofstrasse 3, which in 2015 successfully emerged from a study commissioned by the Baugarten Cooperative, unifies all of the aspects of the contemporary construction of additions as noted. In terms of urban design, its height matches that of its lakeside neighbors, and it forms a powerful pendant to the dome of the Old Stock Exchange. In a sociocultural sense, it satisfies the aforementioned collective aspiration through the extra-height floors with their communal functions and terrace garden. In the interior, light-flooded spaces open up, their organizational structure interlocked with that of the external expression. Within the context of the "series of decisions," it stands within an historical succession, to which the modernist 1932 Witmer & Senn remodeling of the 1880 Stock Exchange building erected by former Semper student Albert Müller, already belonged. And in relation to ambiguity and multivalence, the newly transformed project represents exactly the "new unity, that a fully complete work describes," at the same time belonging to the past as well as to the present. The existing wall panels between the group of small-scale openings facing Bahnhofstrasse were designed as striking pilasters. At the point where they carry the roof to the sky, these were given a capital-like profile using the simplest means. Through the oversized, slightly recessed glazing, the vertical extension has an effect that is light and heavy

25

26

Simultaneous affiliations: vertical extension and rebuilding of Birmanngasse 47 in Basel, by sabarchitekten, 2016; model image and realized street façade.

151

at the same time. At the corner where the panel-like character of the pilasters reveals their thin form, the hierarchy of both façades is defined. The one enhances the static continuity of the Bahnhofstrasse space, while the other appears on Börsenstrasse as a striking, symmetrical figure in dialog with the historic cupola tower. With the simplest means it was possible to put the old and new together in a symbiotic relationship. Thanks to the sublimity of its new proportions, and its role as a model for the contemporary translation of historic themes, this extension, which is not yet built but circulating on the Internet, can no longer fall out of our collective awareness.

We now carry this type of Rorschach test to its conclusion through a final case study: the vertical addition to the Stadthaus on Birmannsgasse in Basel by sabarchitekten.[30] How profane, oddly proportioned, and imperfect would the old house with its two stories and varying window widths appear if it were not for the fine adjustments of the two-story extension, which combines the whole into an expressive showpiece front, where each old and new element has its precise meaning? Through the stucco-covered wood structure of the vertical extension, the historic window frames were reduced to slightly recessed, subdued white surfaces above the metal-clad wood windows. The former attic windows were transformed into ornamental balustrade coverings for the new windows of the vertical extension. These are simultaneously above and below, belonging to the old and the new. From the perspective of construction as well, this simultaneous affiliation with different systems could be turned into synergetic hybrids, through the integration of different, classically separated building methods, thus enriching future developments, not only in the area of steel construction, but more generally in the field of vertical extensions. Intelligently composed hybrids, such as those being studied within the Institute of Constructive Design for several years now, introduce characteristics inherent in the respective material into the structural concept to reciprocal effect, thus resulting in new forms of expression, both in spatial terms and in the external composition.[31]

27

This is exactly what the area of vertical extension—as well as the field of architecture in general—should be about: searching for the familiar and the traditional, beyond the banal and conventional, and integrating these into a multitude—i. e., surprisingly ambiguous and multivalent—of interrelationships. "Design is a progressive series of decisions which remain detectable by the modifications of the system and by their superpositions"; and so we come to Hermann Czech in the conclusion that, "The result can nevertheless be ostensibly simple, when all superpositions align—on closer observation, they reveals their complexity through a vibration."[32]

28

27 Transformation on Schaffhauserplatz in Zurich: vertical extension project by Lukas Küng, Chair of Peter Märkli, EHTZ, 2002/03.
28 Ambiguity and multivalence through vertical extensions: project for the transformation of the Old Stock Exchange on the corner of Bahnhofstrasse and Börsenstrasse in Zurich, by Peter Märkli; study commissioned by the Baugarten Cooperative, 2015.

1   The reference to the new reading of the brilliant essay by Hermann Czech is thanks to the following publication: Österreichischen Gesellschaft für Architektur (ed.), *UM_BAU 29. Umbau. Theorien zum Bauen im Bestand* (Basel: 2017); here Andreas Vass comments on Czech's Text "Der Umbau" (1989) and puts it in context with excerpts from other texts by Czech. "Der Umbau" was first published in Burkhardt Rukschcio and Graphische Sammlung Albertina (eds.), *Adolf Loos* (Vienna: 1989); the essay was then republished in an improved and expanded version of the 1977 anthology published by Löcker Wögenstein, *Zur Abwechselung. Ausgewählte Schriften* (Vienna: 1996). Quote taken from *Zur Abwechslung,* ibid., p. 78.

2   *Werk, Bauen + Wohnen* 1/2 (2017).

3   Hermann Czech, "Wohnbau und Althaus" (1985), in *Zur Abwechslung* (see note 1), p. 107.

4   See text by Daniel Stockhammer in this volume: "New Construction Dressed in an Old Coat: Philipp Jakob Manz's 'Lighting Architecture' for the Salamander Shoe Factory in Kornwestheim, 1927," pp. 40–43.

5   See text by Matteo Iannello in this volume: "Constructing Vertical Extensions: Reassessing Italian Postwar Modernism," pp. 52–62.

6   See text by Martin Tschanz in this volume: "Taming the Future in the Tube: The Design for the Extension of the Kunstakademie Düsseldorf by Karl Wimmenauer, Lyubo-Mir Szabo, and Ernst Kasper in 1968," pp. 96–102.

7   See text by Lorenzo De Chiffre in this volume: "The Psychology of the High-Flyer—On the Vertical Extension of Vienna since Deconstructivism," pp. 85–93.

8   See text by Patric Furrer in this volume: "*Forme forte* and the Picturesque Manner of Vertical Extension at the Turn of the Millennium," pp. 115–121.

9   See Marie Antoinette Glaser and Henriette Steiner, "HausOrdnungen," in *trans 21* (Oct. 2012), pp. 74–83. Here the authors write about a picture from Charles Bertall's, "Cinq étages du monde parisien," in *Le Diable à Paris,* vol. 2 (Paris: 1846): "For him [Charles Bertall], the urban dwelling house contained all of the representatives of the social spectrum of the city. He shows the house as a microcosm. The social and economic organization of the house follows the floors, and at the same time is an illustration of the overall social structure of modern France. This tableau shows different types of households with their occupants, and how they are ordered in the house as well as urban space, through the difference in floors."

10 EPFL, LABEX (Atelier Staufer & Hasler), "Mon aire – mon repos, Aufstockungen in Lausanne," 2nd year semester project (2009); see Atelier Staufer & Hasler, Institut d'architecture de l'EPF de Lausanne (eds.), *Recherche et expérimentation / Suchen und Forschen – LABEX 2007–2011* (Lausanne: 2011), pp. 36–37.

11 Hermann Czech, "Zur Abwechslung" (1973), in *Zur Abwechslung* (see note 1), p. 78.

12 See text by Yves Dreier in this volume: "Geneva—for Centuries, an Experimental Laboratory for Vertical Urban Development," pp. 25–36.

13 Cf. Jean-Claude Maissen and Markus Peter, *Freilager Zürich* (Zurich: 2016).

14 Cf. jury report of the building department of the city of Zurich: https://www.stadt-zuerich.ch/hbd/de/index/ hochbau/wettbewerbe/abgeschlossene_wettbewerbe/ ewz-areal-herdern.html (accessed August 31, 2017).

15 Hermann Czech, "Mehrschichtigkeit" (1977), in *Zur Abwechslung* (see note 1), p. 79.

16 "Über den Dächern," Masterstudio, IKE, 2006 (lecturers: Astrid Staufer, Beat Waeber), and, "Urbane Dachlandschaft heute – Stadtentwicklung in der Vertikalen," Masterstudio, IKE, 2009 (lecturers: Marc Loeliger, Beat Waeber); "Untersuchungen im Rahmen der Forschungsstudie für die Stadt Zürich." The research team included, among others, Matthias Bräm, Patric Furrer, Marc Loeliger, Astrid Staufer, Beat Waeber, and Christoph Wieser.

17 The revised Kantonales Planungs- und Baugesetz (PBG) of 1990 promotes rooftop living.

18 Patric Furrer, "Wohnen über den Dächern – starre Regeln helfen nicht weiter," in *Werk, Bauen + Wohnen,* 1/2 (2017), p. 31.

19 Project description of the rooftop dwelling on Günthergasse in Vienna, description for internal office use by Hermann Czech, Vienna.

20 Hermann Czech, "Mehr Licht" (1964), in *Zur Abwechslung* (see note 1), p. 19.

21 Hermann Czech, "Der Umbau," as well as excerpts from the chapters "Der methodische Aspekt" and "Der kulturelle Aspekt" (1989), ibid., pp. 127, 126

22 See text by Rahel Hartmann, "Chirurgischer Eingriff statt kosmetisches Face-lifting," in *tec21, 7* (2003), pp. 7–12.

23 Andreas Vass, "UM_BAU 29. Umbau. Theorien zum Bauen im Bestand," in ibid., p. 13.

24 See "Gästehaus Science City," in *tec21, 42–43* (2007), p. 8.

25 Martin Josephy, "Oben ist anders," in *Werk, Bauen + Wohnen,* 1/2 (2017), pp. 44–48.

26 Ricardo Joss, "Bericht zum Begleitfach Soziologie," text excerpt from the diploma thesis study, HS 2016.

27 In his text, "Grossstädtische Architektur," Czech interestingly also mentioned the Torre Velasca: "A symbol emerges here, not through formal endeavors, but rather through the sovereignty of thought." Hermann Czech, "Grossstädtische Architektur" (1964), in *Zur Abwechslung* (see note 1), p. 78.

28 Hermann Czech, "Der Umbau" in *Zur Abwechslung* (see note 1), p. 126.

29 See Märkli (Professor for Architecture, ETH Zürich), *Themen/Semesterarbeiten 2002–2015,* Chantal Imoberdorf, ed., exhib. cat., (Zurich: 2016).

30 See Bernard Zurbuchen, "La question de l'echelle et de son contexte immediate," in *Matières – cahier annuel du Laboratoire de théorie et d'histoire* 2 (LTH2), ed. by l'Institut d'architecture et de la ville de l'Ecole polytechnique fédérale de Lausanne (Lausanne: 2016), pp. 78–79.

31 See text by Patric Fischli-Boson in this volume: "On the New Potentials of Steel Construction," pp. 157–160.

32 Hermann Czech, "Einige weitere Entwurfsgedanken" (1980), in *Zur Abwechslung* (see note 1), p. 81.

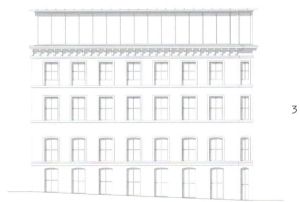

1–6 Story-addition project by Ion Kohler, João Fernandes Silva, and Aliesch Martin, Constructive Research masterclass, ZHAW 2016.

HOW TO BUILD ON?

On the New Potentials of Steel Construction

Patric Fischli-Boson

What can steel do today, what does steel want to be? Steel makes possible an architecture of freedom, and forms its foundation. This freedom already existed in 1851 in Joseph Paxton's Crystal Palace. "Clear construction is the backbone of everything and makes the open plan possible," Ludwig Mies van der Rohe proclaimed, acknowledging the existing advantages of steel as building material, even if he did not limit his own principles to building methods or materials.[1] The freedom of the pioneers was more than just a play of fluid spatial effect.

STEEL CONSTRUCTION IN PLANNING AND FABRICATION

The fact is that the development of "free architecture" has followed a different course. The free plan in steel was only realized in a limited number of building projects. Between the world wars these were largely supplanted by reinforced concrete. Mies left Berlin in 1937, emigrated to Chicago and resuscitated the Chicago School founded by Louis Sullivan. This resulted in the creation of the groundbreaking projects of the great Mies van der Rohe. His architecture was closely linked to what steel as a building material could achieve at that time. The "steel profile" as an essential component of the Miesian corner was introduced as a lineal element, freely combined with secondary elements. The manner in which Mies assembled the profile and articulated it with elements such as glass, masonry, or sheet metal, corresponded to the principle of design dependent upon construction, recalling the post and lintel construction of earlier eras. Steel can thus "stand," "span," "branch," and "connect," as it has been able to do for 150 years.[2] But what new perspectives can it offer?

Steel is not ornament, rather much more the concrete realization of rhythm and tension. Mies declared that, "Architecture starts when you

1   Arne Petter Eggen and Bjorn Normann Sandaker, *Stahl in der Architektur: Konstruktive und gestalterische Verwendung* (Stuttgart: 1996), p. 10.
2   Ibid., p. 13.

4

5

6

HOW TO BUILD ON?

carefully put two bricks together. There it begins."[3] Frank Lloyd Wright remarked that the new materials were able to "destroy the box."[4] Steel thus makes possible an architecture of freedom, that is, the freedom of choice. This choice is often closely bound to the economic production of construction. At this juncture, freedom was curtailed, for the freedom of form ran counter to costs, thus often remaining a dream in a blueprint. This publication presents proponents of deconstructivism, who not only dream this dream, rather they also carried it out, but more as an exception than a rule. This freedom is, or always has been, subject to financial constraints.

The progressive industrialization of construction processes, in particular of steel construction, encourages economically interesting methods and building practices. The freedom once dreamt of is now possible in greater dimensions. Through digital planning and digital fabrication, it is no longer critical if a joint is manufactured and installed identically in great numbers, or on an individual basis. The BIM (Building Information Modelling) and SBA (Steel Beam Assembler) programs offer unheard of possibilities for realizing high quality architectural as well as economical vertical extensiosn in steel. A sensible treatment of the new options offers the potential for the birth of a new architectural vocabulary. Jean Prouvé had developed the first concepts in the area of industrial prefabrication; his prototypes still stand today as models for further constructive development. However, it is surprising that almost seventy years had to pass since the publication of *Wendepunkt im Bauen* by Konrad Wachsmann before a turning point in building could actually be reached.[5]

INTELLIGENTLY COMPOSED HYBRIDS

Contingent upon time resources, new designs may be arrived at through materials and methods that form new structural framing principles and spatial experiences. The field of intelligently composed hybrids, where steel synergistically interacts with other materials, also promises potential for innovation. An example from the Constructive Research masterclass at ZHAW, where this area has long been researched, demonstrates possibilities by way of example.[6]

The goal of this structural framing design was to achieve a vertical extension with as little as possible additional loading, while limiting the structural load to the central wall of an existing late-nineteenth-century house, without thus bearing on the façade. Against this background, students developed the thesis that conventional horizontally stacked wood decking could be partially strengthened with steel sheets. Wood is especially suited to

---

3   Cf: http://www.stadtsatz.de/zitat-mies-van-der-rohe-moderne-architektur (accessed: Dec. 9, 2017). This quote from Mies von der Rohe stems from his time at the Illinois Institute of Technology (IIT) 1959.

4   Eggen and Sandaker, *Stahl in der Architektur* (see note 1), p. 14.

5   Konrad Wachsmann, *Wendepunkt im Bauen* (Wiesbaden: 1959).

6   The Institute of Constructive Design explored hybrid steel construction in the Constructive Research masterclass of 2016 (directed by Alexis Ringli, Patric Furrer, and Patric Fischli-Boson). The following description is based on an evaluation report by Patric Furrer.

compression, and steel to tensile loading. Thus the steel sheets could support thinner, weight-saving wooden decking by compensating for the deficit in tensile stress. The decks were made from horizontally stacked wood decking of partially-fabricated elements held together with wooden dowels and reinforced with steel sheets. The latter were placed where the stress is greatest, that is, in the middle of the area and not at the loading points. The joints, specifically the support points, are thus in a surprising way "tectonically relieved." The supporting elements were configured in reaction to the unconventional expression resulting from the hybrid decking. Their flanges, located far from the loading points, are thus optimal against buckling, and are not continued from the floor to the capital, thus further relieving the joints. The flanges of the vertical supports and the steel sheets of the decking appear to "float" in the space, an expression that derived more from the distribution of forces in the individual elements than from the joints.

The project thus manifests itself as one of those "support structures that does not fulfil its function in concealment, directing the load as directly as possible to the ground; but rather out of this existential theme, this drama, it makes architecture."[7]

7   Cf. Editorial of *Werk, Bauen + Wohnen,* 5 (2009), p. 3.

THE AUTHORS

Jürg Conzett studied Structural Engineering at the EPF Lausanne and the ETH Zürich. After working for Peter Zumthor's office, he started teaching wood construction at HTW Chur and founded his own engineering office. In 2011 Conzett taught at Harvard University. He is a partner at Conzett Bronzini Partner AG and has received numerous awards.

Roger Diener studied at ETH Zürich and EPF Lausanne, under Aldo Rossi and Luigi Snozzi, among others. He took over his father's office in 1980. After guest professorships at EPFL, Harvard University and several different universities in Vienna, Amsterdam, and Copenhagen, he held a professorship for design at EPFL from 1987 to 1989. Fm 1999 to 2015 he was a professor at ETHZ and taught and published his work in collaboration with Marcel Meili, Jacques Herzog, and Pierre de Meuron at the ETH Studio Basel. He has received numerous awards, including the Grande Médaille d'Or, the Prix Meret Oppenheim, and the Heinrich Tessenow Medal.

Lorenzo De Chiffre studied Architecture at the Royal Danish Academy of Fine Arts in Copenhagen and the UEL in London. He has been a lecturer and researcher at TU Vienna at the Department of Building Construction and Design since 2011 and also completed his PhD there in 2016 on the "Viennese terrace house."

Yves Dreier is an architect ETH FAS SIA SWB. He graduated from ETH Zürich in 2004 and in 2008 became a co-founder and partner of Dreier Frenzel architecture + communication in Lausanne. Along with his work as an architect, Dreier is an architecture critic for professional outlets and a member of the editorial board of *Werk, Bauen + Wohnen.* He was a research assistant at EPF Lausanne from 2008 to 2015 and president of the section Romandie of the Swiss Werkbund from 2007 to 2012.

Patric Fischli-Boson studied Structural Engineering at the HSR in Rapperswil. Since 2015, he has directed the Swiss Center for Steel Construction in Zurich and Lausanne. Together with Christoph Büeler, he runs an engineering office in Schwyz. He presides over the SIA's structural engineers' professional group, and has been a lecturer in architecture at the ZHAW since 2016.

Patric Furrer studied Architecture at the ZHAW, the UdK in Berlin, and the UPV in Valencia. He is a research associate at the IKE, and together with Andreas Jud runs the firm of Furrer Jud Architects in Zurich.

Matteo Iannello studied Architecture at the University of Palermo. He completed his PhD on architectural history and built heritage conservation in 2012. He has been a researcher at the University of Venice (IUAV) and has collaborated with the National Museum of 21st-Century Arts in Rome and the Center for High Studies into Visual Arts in Milan. His research focuses on architecture and engineering of the 20th century, and he has been conducting research at the Archive of the Modern at the Accademia di architettura Mendrisio since 2017.

Daniel Meyer studied structural engineering at the ETH Zurich and is co-founder of the firm Dr. Lüchinger + Meyer in Zurich. He is a lecturer at the ZHAW, is also involved in research and serves on numerous committees.

François Renaud studied Architecture at ETH Zürich. After working as an architect in Stockholm, Tel Aviv and Basel, he established his own office together with Franz Engler. At the same time, he worked as a research assistant at ETHZ and as lecturer at the HTA Biel. He has been a lecturer at ZHAW since 2003 and in charge of the architecture degree from 2003 to 2009.

Astrid Staufer studied Architecture at ETH Zurich. Together with Thomas Hasler she has run the architectural firm Staufer & Hasler in Frauenfeld since 1994, and has held a double professorship with him at the TU Vienna since 2011. Since 2015, she has also headed the IKE at the ZHAW, since 2017 together with Andreas Sonderegger. From 2009 to 2016 she was president of the editorial committee of *Werk, Bauen + Wohnen.*

Daniel Stockhammer graduated from the architecture schools of Zurich, Vienna, and Winterthur. After completing his Master's thesis in the ETH Studio Basel under Jacques Herzog and Pierre de Meuron, he started working for their office, while also teaching and completing his PhD at ETHZ. He works as an architect in Zurich and conducts research in the areas of construction techniques and history. He was a research associate at the IKE from 2016 to 2017 and has been teaching design and construction in St. Gallen since 2017.

Martin Tschanz graduated and received his PhD from the Department of Architecture at ETH Zürich. He was a research assistan at the gta Institute and editor at different architecture journals such as *Archithese* und *Werk, Bauen + Wohnen.* He teaches architecture theory, history, and criticism at ZHAW and his writings are regularly published in different professional outlets. In 2015 he published the book *Die Bauschule am Eidgenössischen Polytechnikum Zürich.*

IMAGE CREDITS

INTRODUCTION—
DANIEL STOCKHAMMER

Fig. 1: *Flugzeug G38 (D-2000),* Dessau, Hugo Junkers, 1929 (© Archiv Bernd Junkers, inv. no. ABJ_590_J38_035; photo: anonymous)

Fig. 2: *Flugzeug G38, (D-2500),* Dessau, Hugo Junkers, 1931 (© Archiv Bernd Junkers, inv. no. ABJ_558_034; photo: anonymous

Fig. 3: *Grand Hotel,* Nuremberg, probably 1912 (uncirculated postcard (private); Urania, Graphisches Institut Berlin)

Fig. 4: *Nürnberg Grandhotel—Palast Hotel Fürstenhof,* Nuremberg, 1937 (uncirculated postcard (private); S. Soldan'sche Verlagsbuchhandlung (A. Zemsch), Nuremberg)

Fig. 5: *Hotel am Zoo und Kurfürsten-Keller,* Berlin, c. 1930 (postcard sent on Oct. 9, 1936 (private); KViB)

Fig. 6: *Hotel am Zoo,* Berlin, vertical extension by Paul Baumgarten, 1957 (Akademie der Künste, Berlin, Paul-Baumgarten-Archiv, Nr. 42 F. 63/50; photo: Orgel-Köhne © bpk/Liselotte und Armin Orgel-Köhne)

Fig. 7: *La caisse d'epargne de France,* Paris, Édouard Albert, 1956 (© Agence Roger-Viollet; photo: Janine Niepce)

Fig. 8: *Grand Hotel Colosseo,* Rome, photo montage, Superstudio, 1969 (© MAXXI Museo nazionale delle arti del XXI secolo, Roma MAXXI Architettura Collection, Superstudio Archive, inv. no. 20158)

Fig. 9: *Aufstockungsprojekt Wohnhaus Ermatinger,* Brunnadern SG, Daniel Stockhammer, 2011 (photo: © Daniel Stockhammer)

GENEVA—
YVES DREIER

Cover image: La fontaine, Place de Saint-Gervais, Genève (© BGE Centre iconographie Genève, négatif argentique noir-blanc, download at http://www.notrehistoire.ch; photo: anonymous)

Fig. 1: Quelques maisons du côté impair, La rue de Coutance, Genève, (© BGE Centre iconographie Genève, négatif argentique noir-blanc, download at http://www.notrehistoire.ch; photo: anonymous)

Fig. 2: Place de Saint-Gervais, Genève, c. 1914 (© BGE Centre iconographie Genève, négatif plaque 9 × 12, download at http://www.notrehistoire.ch; photo: Alfred Fradel)

Fig. 3: Carte indicative selon l'article 23 alinéa 4 LCI, accord sur les nouvelles hauteurs d'immeubles, press conference, June 5, 2007, p. 11, République et Canton de Genève, download at http://www.ge.ch/dale/presse-conferences.asp (© Etat de Genève)

Fig. 4 / Fig. 5: Immeuble Place du Cirque, Geneva, BASSICARELLA Architectes (© yves-andre.ch)

Fig. 6 / Fig. 7: Fédération des Entreprises Romandes, Geneva (© Architectes Giorgio Bello, Aydan Yurdakul, François Maurice)

Fig. 8: Carte du potentiel de surélévation selon la loi L10088 (Cecilia Juliano: Introduire la mixité en densifiant des équipements publics. Une strategie pour développer la ville. Prof. Bruno Marchand, EPFL Énoncé théorique de Master 2014, p. 31, download at http://www.archivesma.epfl.ch)

Fig. 9 / Fig. 10: Photomontage avec simulation des nouveaux gabarits de surélévation (existant-nouveau), accord sur les nouvelles hauteurs d'immeubles, press conference, June 5, 2007, pp. 12–13, République et Canton de Genève download at http://www.ge.ch/dale/presse_conferences.asp (© Etat de Genève)

NEW CONSTRUCTION
DRESSED IN AN OLD COAT—
DANIEL STOCKHAMMER

Cover image: Salamander Stammwerk, Kornwestheim, Philipp Jakob Manz, c. 1955 (© Wirtschaftsarchiv Baden-Württemberg, WABW B 150 Fotomappe "Werk 1 Kornwestheim"; photo: H. Moser Kornwestheim)

Fig. 1: Baustelle Aufstockung Hundertmeterbau, Kornwestheim, Philipp Jakob Manz, 1927 (image taken from: Konstanty Gutschow and Hermann Zippel, Umbau, Stuttgart: Julius Hoffmann Verlag, 1932, p. 95.)

Fig. 2: Vogelperspektive der Salamander Schuhfabrik in Kornwestheim, watercolor, anonymous, c. 1920 (private collection; photo: © IMMOVATION-Unternehmensgruppe)

Fig. 3: Salamander Schuhfabrik, Situationsplan (image taken from: Konstanty Gutschow and Hermann Zippel, Umbau, Stuttgart: Julius Hoffmann Verlag, 1932, p. 94)

Fig. 4: Fotomontage mit Bauzustand 1927 (image taken from: Konstanty Gutschow and Hermann Zippel, Umbau, Stuttgart: Julius Hoffmann Verlag, 1932, p. 95)

Fig. 5: Salamander-Schuhfabrik A.-G., Kornwestheim, Philipp Jakob Manz, c. 1930 (postcard sent on Oct. 8,1938 (private); Foto-Feil, Kornwestheim)

CONSTRUCTING VERTICAL EXTENSIONS–
MATTEO IANNELLO

Cover image: Loro e Parisini, Milan, Luigi
Caccia Dominioni, c. 1957 (©Archivio Luigi Caccia
Dominioni, Milan; photo: anonymous)
Fig. 1: Sopraelevazione del Villino Alatri, Rome,
Mario Ridolfi, c. 1950 (©Accademia Nazionale di San
Luca, Rome, perspective view, 12 × 15 cm; photo:
anonymous, CD 83(I/12)
Fig. 2: Sopraelevazione del villino Alatri a Roma,
schizzo prespettico della sopraelevazione su Via
Paisiello angolo Via Bellini, Mario Ridolfi, c. 1948
(©Accademia Nazionale di San Luca, Roma, exterior
view, CD 83/I/14)
Fig. 3: Sopraelevazione del villino Alatri a Roma,
schizzo pianta fondazioni quota 12.00, Mario Ridolfi,
July 22, 1948 (©Accademica Nazionale di San Luca,
Rome, CD 83/II/108)
Fig. 4: Progetto di rigostruzione e sopraelevazione
del fabbricato Eredi Celi a Messina, prospettiva,
Roberto Calandra (©Archivio Roberto Calandra,
Palermo, R.C.23A.1.4)
Fig. 5: Progetto di rigostruzione e sopraelevazione
del fabbricato Eredi Celi a Messina, prospetti,
Roberto Calandra, 1949/50 (©Archivio Roberto
Calandra, Palermo, R.C.23A.1.3.)
Fig. 6: Progetto di rigostruzione e sopraeleva zione
del fabbricato Eredi Celi a Messina, pianta primo
piano/schema di sezione, Roberto Calandra, 1949/50
(©Archivio Roberto Calandra, Palermo, R.C.23A.1.1)
Fig. 7: Progetto di rigostruzione e sopraelevazione
del fabbricato Eredi Celi a Messina, pianta secondo
piano/piano attico, Roberto Calandra, 1949/50
(©Archivio Roberto Calandra, Palermo, R.C.23A.1.2)
Fig. 8: Loro e Parisini, Milan, Luigi Caccia
Dominioni, c. 1957 (©Archivio Luigi Caccia
Dominioni, Milan; photo: anonymous)
Fig. 9: Loro e Parisini, Milan, Luigi Caccia
Dominioni, c. 1957 (©Archivio Luigi Caccia
Dominioni, Milan, inv. no. 3311; photo: anonymous)
Fig. 10: Loro e Parisini, Milan, Luigi Caccia
Dominioni, c. 1957 (©Archivio Luigi Caccia
Dominioni, Milano; photo: anonymous)
Fig. 11: Loro e Parisini, Milan, Luigi Caccia
Dominioni, c. 1957 (©Archivio Luigi Caccia
Dominioni, Milan, inv. no. 3275; photo: anonymous)

DESIGN THROUGH
CONSTRUCTIVE THINKING–
DANIEL STOCKHAMMER

Cover image: Aufstockung Architekturabteilung
TH Hannover, Friedrich Spengelin and Horst
Wunderlich, c. 1970 (photo: ©Photo Lill, Hannover)
Fig. 1: Geschäftsbücherfabrik J. C. König &
Ebhardt, Hannover, Heinrich G. L. Frühling, graphic
art (probably lithograph), anonymous, 1895
(©Historisches Museum Hannover, Bildarchiv,
inv. no. 023367)
Fig. 2: Teilzerstörung an der Schlosswender Strasse,
Hannover, 1941 (©Historisches Museum Hannover,
Bildarchiv, inv. no. 061719; photo: anonymous)
Fig. 3: Königsworther Platz (damals Horst-Wessel-
Platz) mit der Geschäftsbücherfabrik J. C. König &
Ebhardt, Hannover, Heinrich G. L. Frühling, c. 1930
(©Historisches Museum Hannover, Bildarchiv,
inv. no. 034844; photo: Adolf Schuhmacher)
Fig. 4: Architekturabteilung TH Hannover (heute
Leibniz Universität), Friedrich Spengelin and Horst
Wunderlich, image taken around 1990 (©Leibniz-
Universität, inv. no. Img0041; photo: anonymous)
Fig. 5: Kopfbau der ehemaligen Architekturab-
teilung, Leibniz Universität Hannover, Friedrich
Spengelin and Horst Wunderlich, image taken in
2014 (photo: Christian A. Schröder, public domain,
https://commons.wikimedia.org/File:Former_printing_
plant_Koenig_Ebhardt_Schlosswender_Strasse_
Koenigsworther_Platz_Hannover_Germany.jpg,
original in color)
Fig. 6: Innenaufnahme Empore, Aufstockung
Architekturfakultät TH Hannover, Friedrich Spengelin
and Horst Wunderlich, c. 1970 (photo: ©Photo Lill,
Hannover)
Fig. 7: Blick vom ersten Aufstockungsgeschoss
in die Empore darüber, Aufstockung Architekturfakultät TH Hannover, Friedrich Spengelin and Horst
Wunderlich, c. 1970 (photo ©Photo Lill, Hannover)

THE PSYCHOLOGY OF THE HIGH-FLYER–
LORENZO DE CHIFFRE

Cover image: Überbauung Wien, photo
montage, Hans Hollein, 1960 (photo ©Centre
Pompidou, MNAM-CCI, Dist. RMN-Grand
Palais/Georges Meguerditchian)
Fig. 1: Dachausbau Falkestrasse, Vienna, Coop
Himmelb(l)au, 1998 (Technische Universität Wien,
Institut für Gebäudelehre; photo: Christina Gruber)
Fig. 2: Dachausbau Falkestrasse, Vienna, Coop
Himmelb(l)au, date unknown (photo: ©Gerald
Zugmann, Wien/www.zugmann.com)

Fig. 3: Dachausbau Falkestrasse, Vienna, Coop Himmelb(l)au, date unknown (photo: © Duccio Malagamba, P_8401_F562_DM)
Fig. 4: Dachausbau Falkestrasse, Vienna, floorplan (© Coop Himmelb(l)au, Vienna)
Fig. 5: Dachausbau Falkestrasse, Vienna, section (© Coop Himmelb(l)au, Vienna)
Fig. 6: Dachausbau Seilergasse, Vienna, RLP Rüdiger Lainer + Partner, 1995 (© Architekturzentrum Wien, Collection, inv. no. 5527-b; photo: Margherita Spiluttini)
Fig. 7: Dachausbau Seilergasse, Vienna, RLP Rüdiger Lainer + Partner, 1995 (© Architekturzentrum Wien, Collection, inv. no. 5529-b; photo: Margherita Spiluttini)
Fig. 8: Dachausbau Seilergasse, Vienna, RLP Rüdiger Lainer + Partner, 1995 (© Architekturzentrum Wien, Collection, inv. no. 5530-a; photo: Margherita Spiluttini)
Fig. 9: Dachausbau Seilergasse, Vienna, floorplan (© RLP Rüdiger Lainer + Partner, Vienna)
Fig. 10: Dachausbau Seilergasse, Vienna, section (© RLP Rüdiger Lainer + Partner, Vienna)
Fig. 11: Dachausbau Ray 1, Vienna, Delugan Meissl Associated Architects, probably 2002 (photo: © Delugan Meissl Associated Architects)
Fig. 12: Dachausbau Ray 1, Vienna, Delugan Meissl Associated Architects, probably 2003 (photo: © Rupert Steiner, Vienna, 030403-05)
Fig. 13: Dachausbau Ray 1, Vienna, Delugan Meissl Associated Architects, probably 2003 (photo: © Rupert Steiner, Vienna, 030403-49)
Fig. 14: Dachausbau Ray 1, Vienna, floorplan (© Delugan Meissl Associated Architects)

TAMING THE FUTURE IN THE TUBE—
MARTIN TSCHANZ

Cover image: Projekt zur Aufstockung der Kunstakademie, Düsseldorf, Karl Wimmenauer with Lyubo-Mir Szabo and Ernst Kasper, 1968, photo of model (© Karl-Wimmenauer-Archiv, Deutsches Architekturmuseum, Frankfurt am Main, inv. no. 345-033-099)
Fig. 1: Entwurfsvariante, Aufstockung Kunstakademie, Düsseldorf, Karl Wimmenauer, 1968, felt tip pen on tracing paper (© Karl-Wimmenauer-Archiv, Deutsches Architekturmuseum, Frankfurt am Main, inv. no. 345-033-023)
Fig. 2: Entwurfsvariante, Aufstockung Kunstakademie, Düsseldorf, Karl Wimmenauer, 1968, felt tip pen on tracing paper (© Karl-Wimmenauer-Archiv, Deutsches Architekturmuseum, Frankfurt am Main, inv. no. 345-033-041)

Fig. 3: Entwurfsvariante, Aufstockung Kunstakademie, Düsseldorf, Karl Wimmenauer, 1968, pencil on tracing paper (© Karl-Wimmenauer-Archiv, Deutsches Architekturmuseum, Frankfurt am Main, inv. no. 345-033-024)
Fig. 4: Entwurfsvariante, Aufstockung Kunstakademie, Düsseldorf, Karl Wimmenauer, 1968, pencil and ink on blueprint (© Karl-Wimmenauer-Archiv, Deutsches Architekturmuseum, Frankfurt am Main, inv. no. 345-033-046)
Fig. 5: Konzeptskizze auf axonometrischer Stadtansicht, Düsseldorf, Karl Wimmenauer, 1968, copy (© Karl-Wimmenauer-Archiv, Deutsches Architekturmuseum, Frankfurt am Main, inv. no. 345-033-072)
Fig. 6: Querschnitt, Aufstockung Kunstakademie, Düsseldorf, Karl Wimmenauer with Lyubo-Mir Szabo and Ernst Kasper, 1968, photocopy and drawing (© Karl-Wimmenauer-Archiv, Deutsches Architekturmuseum, Frankfurt am Main, inv. no. 345-033-002)
Fig. 7: Ansichten, Aufsichten, Perspektive und Schnitt, Düsseldorf, Karl Wimmenauer, 1968, etching (© Karl-Wimmenauer-Archiv, Deutsches Architekturmuseum, Frankfurt am Main, inv. no. 345-033-001a)
Fig. 8: Fotomontage mit Architekturmodell, Düsseldorf, Karl Wimmenauer with Lyubo-Mir Szabo and Ernst Kasper, photographic studio of the academy of Mladen Lipecky, 1968 (© Karl-Wimmenauer-Archiv, Deutsches Architekturmuseum, Frankfurt am Main, inv. no. 345-033-088)
Fig. 9: Fotomontage mit Architekturmodell, Düsseldorf, Karl Wimmenauer with Lyubo-Mir Szabo and Ernst Kasper, photographic studio of the academy of Mladen Lipecky, 1968 (© Karl-Wimmenauer-Archiv, Deutsches Architekturmuseum, Frankfurt am Main, inv. no. 345-033-004)

FORME FORTE—
PATRIC FURRER

Cover image: Konzeptmodell Elbphilharmonie, Hamburg, Herzog & de Meuron Basel, 2003 (photo: © Herzog & de Meuron)
Fig. 1: Kubus, Alberto Giacometti, 1933/34 (© Succession Alberto Giacometti / 2019, ProLitteris, Zurich)
Fig. 2: Untitled (Six Cold Rolled Steel Boxes), Donald Judd, 1969 (© Judd Foundation / 2019, ProLitteris, Zurich)
Fig. 3: Haus Bonnin, Eichstätt, Hild und K Architekten Munich, 1996 (photo: © Michael Heinrich, Munich)
Fig. 4 / Fig. 5: CaixaForum, Madrid, Herzog & de Meuron Basel, 2008 (photo: © Iñigo Bujedo-Aguirre)

165

Fig. 6 / Fig. 7: Aufstockung eines Wohnhauses, Toulouse, BAST, Toulouse, 2013 (photo: ©BAST, Toulouse)

Fig. 8: Elbphilharmonie, Hamburg, Herzog & de Meuron Basel, 2017 (photo: ©Maxim Schulz Photographer, Hamburg)

Fig. 9: 100 untitled works in mill aluminum, Marfa, Donald Judd, 1982–86 (photo: ©John Locke, New York)

Fig. 10: Elbphilharmonie, Hamburg, Herzog & de Meuron Basel, 2017 (photo: ©Iwan Baan, Amsterdam)

HISTORY OF MINING,
MINING OF HISTORY—
ROGER DIENER AND JÜRG CONZETT

Cover image: Aussenansicht Projektvorschlag, Aufstockung Kohlenwäsche Zeche Zollverein, Diener & Diener Architekten Basel, 1999, photo montage (©Diener & Diener Architekten, Basel)

Fig. 1: Historische Aussenansicht von Förderturm (links hinten) und Kohlenwäsche (rechts), Zeche Zollverein Schacht 12, Fritz Schupp and Martin Kremmer, c. 1950 (©Anton Meinholz / Fotoarchiv Ruhr Museum)

Fig. 2: Aussenansicht Förderturm mit Projektvorschlag zur Aufstockung der Kohlenwäsche, Zeche Zollverein, Diener & Diener Architekten Basel, 1999, photo montage (©Diener & Diener Architekten, Basel)

Fig. 3: Querschnitt, Projektvorschlag Aufstockung Kohlenwäsche, Zeche Zollverein, Diener & Diener Architekten Basel, 1999 (©Diener & Diener Architekten, Basel)

Fig. 4: Diagramme, Statisches Konzept der Aufstockung, Jürg Conzett, 1999 (©Conzett Bronzini Partner AG, Chur)

Fig. 5: Innenaufnahme bestehende Portalträger in der Kohlenwäsche, Zeche Zollverein, Essen (©Diener & Diener Architekten, Basel)

Fig. 6: Aussenansicht Schachtanlage 12 mit Projektvorschlag zur Aufstockung der Kohlenwäsche, Zeche Zollverein, Essen, 1999, photo montage (©Diener & Diener Architekten, Basel)

WAYS TOWARDS AMBIGUITY—
ASTRID STAUFER

Fig. 1: "Cinq étages du monde parisien," Charles Bertall, in Le Diable à Paris, vol. 2 (Paris 1846), used, among other things, as a cover image by George Perec in La vie, mode d'emploi (Paris: Hachette, 1978).

Fig. 2: Mon aire—mon repos, Aufstockung als Aussenraum, Längsschnitt Bestand und Aufstockung

mit kollektivem Zwischenraum, student projects by Giulia Altarelli, Elsa Beniada, 2009 (photo: ©LABEX Prof. Staufer & Hasler, EPFL)

Fig. 3 / Fig. 4: Vertical Extension Curtain Road, London, Morris + Company, 2010 (photo: ©Jack Hobhouse)

Fig. 5: Conversion and extension, Kanaal, Wijnegem (BE), COUSSÉE & GORIS architecten, 2007–16, model (photo: ©Axel Vervoordt)

Fig. 6: Freilagerareal Zürich-Albisrieden, view from the southwest, Meili, Peter und Partner Architekten, 2016 (photo: ©Georg Aerni)

Fig. 7 / Fig. 8: EWZ Herdern Zürich, commissioned study contribution, Christian Kerez, 2016, structure and positioning models (photos: ©Architekturbüro Christian Kerez)

Fig. 9 / Fig. 10: Studie Urbane Dachlandschaften heute, Ausgangslage und Projekt, student projects by Ivo Hasler, Master Studio 2009 (©ZHAW IKE)

Fig. 11: Dachaufbau/-ausbau, Strassenansicht mit Doppelgaube und Eckterrasse zur Votivkirche, Günthergasse Vienna, Hermann Czech, 2007–11 (photo: ©Gabriele Kaiser)

Fig. 12: Dachaufbau/-ausbau, Innenansicht der Dacheinschnitte und Auswölbungen, Günthergasse Vienna, Hermann Czech, 2007–11 (photo: ©Gerhard Flora, Atelier Czech)

Fig. 13: Dachaufbau/-ausbau, Günthergasse Vienna, Hermann Czech, 2007–11, section (©Atelier Czech)

Fig. 14: Bürogebäude Helvetia vor der Aufstockung, Zürich-Altstetten, Hans von Meyenburg, 1970 (photo: ©Heinrich Helfenstein)

Fig. 15: Aufstockung und Umbau Bürogebäude Helvetia als integral neu gestalteter und aufgestockter Gesamtbaukörper, Zürich Altstetten, Romero & Schäfle, 2001 (photo: ©René Furer)

Fig. 16 / Fig. 17: Aufstockung eines Lagergebäudes des ehemaligen Zollfreilagers am Dreispitz in Münchenstein, Basel, Bjarke Ingels Group, 2016 (photos: ©Laurian Ghinitoiu)

Fig. 18: Praktikumsgebäude, ETH Hönggerberg, Zurich, Albert H. Steiner, 1965 (©ETH-Bibliothek, Bildarchiv, doi.org/10.3932/ethz-a-000013082; photo: anonymous)

Fig. 19: Visualisierung Wettbewerbsprojekt "Schimmelreiter," Aufstockung Gästehaus Science City ETH Hönggerberg, Zurich, Ilg Santer, 2007 (©Ilg Santer, publiziert in tec21 42/43 (2007), p. 8)

Fig. 20: Werkplan, Querschnitt Aufstockung Gästehaus Science City ETH Hönggerberg, Zürich, Ilg Santer, 2007 (©Ilg Santer)

Figs. 21-24: Aufstockung Genossenschaftssiedlung Talbächli, Modell der Aufstockung mit aussenliegender Tragstruktur und Blick aus der